Lessons Learned
from the Bottom of the Stairs

A Story of Faith & Resilience

by
Randy Milliken
as told to
Debbie Johnson

Lessons Learned from the Bottom of the Stairs

Copyright © 2018

Unless otherwise marked, Scripture quotations have been taken from the Holy Bible, New International Version, NIV Copyright 1973, 1978, 1984, 2011 by Biblica, Inc.

ISBN 9781728927183
Printed in the United States of America by Kindle Direct Publishing, www.kdp.amazon.com

Cover design by Megan Etter.

Dedicated to Carolyn Finnell

TABLE of CONTENTS

Table of Contents

ACKNOWLEDGEMENTS

I want to thank several dear friends for helping me bring this book from an idea to reality.

Debbie Johnson for her inspiration, co-writing of portions, organization, and editing.

David Warren for reading the draft and making edits.

Michelle Warren for writing the foreword.

Megan Etter for designing the cover.

Mike Wolff for his inspiration and assistance.

Sandi Rog for her contributions to content.

Kim Sierra for managing the business details.

Jim and Debi Simons for their invaluable assistance with the publication process.

My family and friends for their encouragement and prayers when the task seemed too daunting.

I'm also grateful for so many churches, organizations, and ministries that have blessed me along the way, including Open Door Fellowship, Open Door Ministries, TRYAD, and Joni & Friends.

FOREWORD

I remember the Sundays during Open Door Ministries' Family Room construction project well. Since 2007, my husband David Warren, Director of Open Door Ministries, had talked about a space in the church where Open Door could build community. I remember him saying, "Families hang out in family rooms. We need to build a Family Room!" This shared dream began to unfold with a couple of years of fundraising and construction. Prior to this season, Open Door Fellowship's building was defined by a handicap ramp nearly 50 ft. long to provide wheelchair access to the second floor of the church. Tearing it down was stage one for the construction project. The proposed elevator, which would now go to all three floors, would be the final stage. All we had to do was wait. That sacrificial waiting was most painful for those in wheelchairs, but also for those who loved them.

I remember our family heading to church on Sunday mornings, trudging through the alley-side playground (a makeshift entrance during construction) and up the side stairs to get to the service, and I remember Randy, parked at the bottom. I still get choked up when I recall the feelings I had as we left him weekly to his perch at the bottom of the stairs, easily ascending into the sanctuary to worship together. The reality of wheelchair limitations was starker in that season than ever. Yet, with his decision to "choose joy" as one of his heroes Tim Hansel says, every Sunday Randy faithfully greeted church attendees with a smile on his face, a sincere word from his heart and assurances that he was fine at the bottom of the stairs, learning lesson upon lesson from the Jesus he had trusted and still trusts despite his physical limitations.

If you know Randy, you know his strong, competitive spirit that keeps him showing up to what he believes God is calling him to do. It's that strength that enabled him to faithfully stay in that place regardless of cold weather, construction delays and any other excuse that others might have made to not be there. To know Randy means you know his tender heart that cares about learning and leaning on

Jesus and community, compelling him to share Jesus' love in creative and persistent ways, this book being one!

Randy has always been a gift to the Open Door community and as you'll see in his story, to many other churches and ministries as well. However, those couple of years that he sat at the bottom of the stairs were particularly challenging for me as it seemed glaring that all of Randy's humility and goodness were being tested unfairly. I had lessons to learn through his experience as well. Randy was waiting, learning and listening to the God in whom we both believe, who redeems the broken and hard, refining it beautifully. He has lived life faithfully learning, pushing against easy answers and closing doors, actively allowing God to take whatever He is given and turn it into the gift of life, even what he refers to as the gift of suffering. Randy says, "Suffering is a gift. You give it to God. [Our] job is to surrender, even though God's answers may not be what [we] would have thought."

Randy, you indeed have received a few PhD's in Life! Keep sharing your perspective and mentoring us with your humility, compassion and love. The Body of Christ is richer because of you and your shared desire for us all to be the people God calls us to be, wherever He chooses to place us.

Michelle Ferrigno Warren
Advocacy & Strategic Engagement Director
Christian Community Development Association (CCDA)

Author of *The Power of Proximity*

PREFACE

My name is Randy Milliken. I want to tell you my story through some lessons I've learned over the years. As I look back on my life, the lessons all point in the same direction—COMMUNITY with others and UNITY with my Lord and Savior Jesus Christ.

God gave me the image of "lessons learned from the bottom of the stairs" from where else but the bottom of some stairs…at Open Door Fellowship. You see, I have cerebral palsy. When I first got to Open Door in 1993, I was on crutches and able to carefully climb the stairs by creatively hanging on to my crutches in one hand and the rail on the other side. As I've gotten older, I've gotten weaker. I'm now 60 years old and I depend on an electric wheelchair, but fortunately, Open Door now has an elevator!

Because it had been so hard to get to the upper floors at Open Door during the construction of the Family Room 2015-2016, I often sat at the bottom of the stairs with the door to the sanctuary open to listen to Andy Cannon preach. Andy is Open Door's pastor. I love hearing his sermons so much! It was often very, very cold at the bottom of the stairs. I gained a greater empathy for those who actually live and sleep in the frigid cold.

Open Door Fellowship enthusiastically reaches out to those who live on the streets. They are invited to be a part of the congregation for the purpose of discipleship, not just to make converts. Open Door invites them out of the cold, offering them a cup of coffee and a warm place to hear the gospel and put their faith in Jesus Christ. It also offers them help through its programs and discipleship homes.

At the bottom of the stairs, I witnessed how often the poor with very short attention spans descended the stairs every few minutes, even while Andy was preaching, just to get a few puffs from a cigarette or take a phone call, before going back upstairs.

From the bottom of the stairs, I was inspired to think about life on earth and how Jesus Christ, God the Father, and the Holy Spirit are with us here on earth, yet the things we know and experience here are certainly different from the heavenly perspective. The metaphor I want to use is that of equating life on earth as being downstairs from heaven, just like I was downstairs from where I would prefer to be, which was with the Lord and my brothers and sisters in Christ in the sanctuary. (Fortunately, along the way, I've learned that He is above me, but He's also within me.)

As I share lessons learned from the bottom of the stairs, my hope is to describe my life and the home I grew up in to show you how much of a dreamer I was. Some of these dreams got me into trouble like pornography; others were related to my love for sports. One is a picture of reality and hardship; another about trying to escape reality. The Lord God redeemed those dreams and gave purpose and meaning to them. God used my love for sports to draw me to Himself! Many athletes, some old and retired and others who were active on the field, communicated the gospel of Jesus Christ to me. As a result, I grew to use my love for athletes to communicate the great and mighty love of Jesus Christ back to them.

Although I am single, some of my dreams and fantasies became reality in more ways than one, including being married in a spiritual sense to Jesus Christ! It's amazing, because my desire to have a wife to love and be taken care of by (rather than letting Christ teach me to be a leader at home) nearly caused me to shipwreck my life about thirty-five years ago through attempted suicide!

Some of my dreams merged to become one. Others were set on a different course, yet still have a meaningful purpose. Along the way, I've written lots of poetry, both before and after I gave my life to my Lord in 1979. Some of my poems are included here.

These are my stories…and this is the greater story of the Amazing Love of God the Father and his miraculous Son our Lord and Savior Jesus Christ! Amen.

Lesson Learned: Looking back on my times at the bottom of the stairs, I have learned to pay attention to every situation and find God's lesson in it.

Preface

CHAPTER 1
Lessons of Purpose

My full name is Randall Roy Milliken. Randall was the first name of my father's dad. Roy was the first name of my mother's dad. My family history goes back to Ireland. I know this because my Great Uncle Bill had an Irish accent!

I was born on February 28th, 1958 at Porter Hospital in Englewood, Colorado. I was born six weeks prematurely at 4 lbs. 9 and ¾ oz. I was the first of three children born to my parents, James Randall Milliken and Barbara Jean (Seip) Milliken. My mother always lightheartedly says that Seip is pies spelled backwards! Haha! The name has German roots. Her current last name is Kauffman. She was married briefly and happily to Jerry Kauffman who passed away on, of all things, her birthday, April 21, 2010.

My father's family line takes one step back from Denver to a town near Greeley and Windsor that was given my family surname, Milliken (Colorado). My Great Uncle Kenny was once a Grand Marshall in a parade there. However, I have never been there. Before the town of Milliken, my family history took one step back to the neighboring state of Nebraska. And then back to Pennsylvania and then back to Ireland.

My birth has some amazing adventure associated with it. My mom and dad, both Denver natives, had originally decided to make a life for themselves in California, but the Lord had other plans! (When I say the Lord had other plans, I'm referring to the sovereign hand of God in my life and its events even before I made a conscious choice to acknowledge Him. He knew I would be born with cerebral palsy. He is sovereign.)

My mom was pregnant with me when they first settled in California. My father's father, my Grandpa Randy, had served in the Army Air Forces as a mess hall sergeant. He was given the chance to be a cook at the new Air Force Academy to be located in Colorado Springs, but before that ever happened, he was diagnosed with cancer. My father got a call from family members urging him to come home to Denver right away, so my parents departed for Denver.

In their travels, they went over Monarch Pass. It was snowing very hard and my dad could hardly see anything in front of him. The roads were narrow. He decided to get out of the car and walk ahead while Mom drove the car, so he could provide a line of sight. He told Mom to keep the driver's side window down so she could hear his instructions in case there were trucks coming the other way from around the corner.

They made it safely down from the pass, but as a result of the window being down, my mom became very sick with a cold. She once told me she got so sick that she thought she was going to cough me up!!! She told me this is why I was born six weeks early and very small…and is also why I was born with cerebral palsy. She said once I was born, the cold she had went away almost immediately!! I was the only one of the three children that was held by Grandpa Randy before he passed away. My father told me several years after high school that Grandpa Randy died of cancer related to alcohol abuse.

At six weeks premature, the nurses and doctors said I had a "stridor's cry" because my lungs were underdeveloped. Mom called me her little fighter, because that's what it meant from the very beginning in the incubator; my fists would clench and my whole body would turn red. And really, that describes my whole life. It's been nothing but a battle…a battle to learn to listen to others and a battle to learn to listen to God.

Lesson Learned: Looking back on the circumstances of my birth, I have learned that God has a great plan for my life, even though it had a rocky start.

Lessons of Purpose

CHAPTER 2
Lessons of Family

My sister Brenda was born one year later, on August 22, 1959, and my little sister Lana was born one year after that on October 30, 1960. We lived in what we called The Pink House in Lakewood, Colorado. Mom and Dad and the three of us sometimes went camping in Deckers, Colorado or water skiing at Sloan's Lake. We also went roller skating and Dad would carry us on his shoulders. I know my dad and mom loved us very much!

I was mischievous, the instigator of stuff even though I was on crutches. I would scoot on my fanny to get cereal, digging through to get the prize before my sisters could. Suddenly there was cereal all over the floor!

We used open drawers as a ladder, which we used to get to the bubble gum balls. Mom had smoker's cough, so I would hear her coming when we were into the cereal or bubble gum balls. I would scoot to my bedroom and my sisters would get the spanking. It happened over and over. One day I didn't hear her cough and she caught me! "It was you!" she said. "You brat!"

I spent a lot of time with Mom watching the Denver Bears on television while she knitted me a sweater or made me new Space Man pajamas at the sewing machine. The Denver Bears were a Triple A farm team in the American Association. They were the top farm team of the Washington Senators when I began to follow them on the radio at "KLZ Radio 560 on the Dial." The games always started at 7:55 p.m. with Don Cole and Jack Jolly.

1967 was the year it all started for me. They would broadcast the game on occasional Friday nights with Fred Leo on KWGN Channel 2 and I would get to watch live. I fell in love with some of the players in my mind on the radio, like Jackie Brown, Jeff Burrows, Tom Grieve, and Jim Mason.

When 7:55 p.m. came, I would run to my bedroom and grab a pair of my underwear, which was what I would use as a baseball. If I threw my underwear in the air towards the ceiling and turned my wrist to

5

the right, that was a curveball. If I threw them in the air and turned my wrist to the left, it was a slider. If I put my underwear tightly in my fingertips and threw them in the air as hard as I could, that was my fastball. I would throw my underwear as soon as I heard the announcer say, "And the pitch!" Baseball was the first girl I ever loved. Haha!

Frequently, from the time I was young until I got significantly older, I tried to manipulate circumstances to self-medicate the fear that gripped me. I am almost certain my attempts to self-medicate started with those games on the radio. Later, self-medicating led to addictions.

When my mom was reading the newspaper, it got quiet. Unbearably quiet! She would be at peace, but I would create a rhythm in my head and start tapping a pencil or slapping my hand on the floor. Mom would say, "Sh-h-h-h! Can't you be quiet?" But I was scared. I thought that if it's quiet, it won't be long before the next shoe drops! So at 7:55 p.m. I would head to my bedroom, put the game on the radio, and fantasize pitching as if I was the one on the mound for real.

Lesson Learned: Looking back on my childhood, I have learned that I formed patterns of escape that led to addictions. But down the road, God led me to Himself. My fear and addictions are conquered in Him.

During my early years, Mom would pay me a quarter if I could make my bed well enough for a quarter to bounce on it. She got this idea from her brothers, my Uncles Rick and Al. Uncle Rick was in the Army and Uncle Al was in the Navy. Bouncing a quarter on the bed meant that the bed was made correctly and that there were no wrinkles in the sheets. (And if the quarter bounced, I got to keep it!) As a kid, I used to dream about being in the military like my uncles. I was too young to realize that I couldn't go to the military because of my disability, but I wanted to be like my uncles.

CHAPTER 3
Lessons of Remembrance

This is a tribute to all who have served in the military, including my relatives. My mother told me I couldn't serve but I could thank veterans and honor them in different ways. Since then, it has been on my heart to paint a picture with words to describe what I have seen and what I have read in a creative way. This poetic tribute is just that. It is entitled "A New Leg to Stand On."

Dear Lord,
May this be a tribute to Bert Shepard, who served as a fighter pilot in the Army Air Forces during World War II. May this be a tribute to my namesake, Randall Fremont Milliken, and to my great-uncle, James Robert Seip, both of whom served in the Army Air Forces during World War II. May this be a tribute to my father as I recall our memories together, in life and in sports.

May this be a tribute to the families of everyone who has served in our Armed Forces, past and present, to protect our country, the U.S.A.

Bert Shepard was a first baseman and pitcher in the low minor leagues of the Chicago White Sox baseball organization before becoming a pilot in the Army Air Forces.

In May of 1944, his White Sox got dirty, as soon as his feet hit the floor. If you and I walked a mile in his socks, would there be any doubt that ours would be dirty too? If so, would we, in empathy, be willing to comfort and encourage him with the comfort we have received in Christ if he were singing the blues?
2 Corinthians 1:3-7

Shepard was strafing a caravan of trucks north of Berlin when anti-aircraft fire brought his plane to the ground. Almost before anyone heard a sound, German farmers were approaching him with pitchforks in their hands, and revenge in their hearts. But then as they looked up, a German military doctor was holding them off at gunpoint as he was pulling Shepard, with his mangled right leg, to safety!

He woke up in a German hospital, a prisoner of war, with his right leg removed below the knee. Yet without a beg or even a plea, but with a grateful heart instead, the question that you or I might ask, "Why?" was not entertained. It was left out in the dark and cold where it belongs. Maybe he thought it privately, but through some great inner peace, it was left unsaid. "What have you done for me lately, oh you enemies, who brought me to safety?"

In February1945, Shepard boarded a prisoner exchange ship, and set his sights for home. At Walter Reed Army Hospital, a place devoted to war amputees, he was given a new artificial leg. And there was a flame of hope in his heart to reunite with The Boys of Summer, to make a brand new start.

In March of 1945, the Undersecretary of War Patterson spoke with Shepard and learned of his desire to play baseball again. Mr. Patterson arranged for a tryout in the majors with the Washington Senators. Shepard was given but one chance; one chance is what dreamers dream about and sometimes one chance is all you get. He indeed was able to join the Senators, but was officially listed as a coach.
On August 4, 1945, the Senators were losing the game 14-2 and Bert was called in from the bullpen with the bases full of Red Sox. He struck out George Metkovich to get out of the inning!

Each inning after that was a new beginning. He continued to strafe a caravan of Red Sox batters, throwing any number of pitches; fast balls, change-ups, sliders, curves. He threw five and one-third innings, only allowing one run on three hits!

When he came into the game, he was officially listed as a coach, yet was still an active lieutenant. Throwing pitches from the mound, he used his status in a humble sort of way to lead his Senator teammates. Even though they lost the game, he inspired them and others, through difficulty and hardship, to reach for the stars!

This would be the last time he would pitch. The next public appearance he made was at Griffith Stadium, a few weeks later, on August 31st. He appeared with Secretary Patterson along with

General Omar Bradley. He was awarded the Distinguished Flying Cross for bravery and conduct in battle in a ceremony at the stadium.

In 1946 he made a public tour of centers for war amputees. He also worked first at IBM and then as a Safety Engineer and Employment Specialist for the Handicapped at Hughes Aircraft. He died in 2008.

When he stepped on the mound on August 4, 1945, he may have entered the game with a brand new leg to stand on, but in the end, through his life, he inspired many hearts to appreciate the contentment of having two legs to stand on!

(The information about Bert Shepard is taken from an article written in the New York Times in June 2008 by Richard Goldstein.)

Lesson Learned: In so many ways, the road of life is paved by the steps of those who have gone before. I am so grateful for my relatives and other heroic, inspirational figures from the past.

CHAPTER 4
Lessons of Wounds

So back to my mom. Mom patiently worked with me and encouraged me all along the way. If I helped her in the kitchen, she would spice up the opportunity by telling me we could make Jell-O if I would dry the dishes. We would have great talks and laugh! I loved my mom just like any other little boy, but we were very close partially due to circumstances at home.

Mom hung a picture over my bed as a child, which was of Jesus standing at the door knocking, from Revelation 3:20. "Behold, I stand at the door and knock. Whoever opens the door, I will go in and eat with him and he with me." I lost that picture in my childhood, but later my dear friend, Gayle Barrett, found a larger version and gave it to me. It hangs above the door to my room now.

Mom and Dad had arguments that woke me up at night. (I don't know the experience of my two sisters as it pertains to this. I do know my sisters and I had trouble at night with bed wetting but for the most part, all I can do is speak for myself. Some of it was a bladder control issue associated with cerebral palsy. Other times it was because I was lazy. And still other times, because I wanted to play with my friends rather than go to the bathroom. It seemed that I had just been there, and it took extra effort to go back again!)

This was difficult on my mom and dad. Dad was a firm disciplinarian and I was frequently afraid of him. I knew he loved me, yet his mood swings confused me. When I reached my high school years, I learned that he struggled with various addictions, mainly alcohol. I experienced along with my sisters how alcohol impacted our family history.

He was a firm disciplinarian, but in sincere love and fairness to him and the relationship we have today, his disciplinary approach was learned behavior. You can lead a horse to water, but you can't make it drink. Even tough horses like Dad or I get a chance to drink Living Water if we will acknowledge Jesus Christ as our Lord and Savior. See John chapter 4 about the Woman at the Well and John 3:16.

Lessons Learned from the Bottom of the Stairs

My mom and my dad divorced when I was around six or seven years old. All I wanted was to have them back together again. I could not wrap my mind around why they went separate ways, but they did.

When they separated, Dad put the three of us on the front lawn and told us the bad news; Mom was gone! Ironically, that was also the place where so many times Mom read stories to us. After Dad got stronger in his sobriety, he told us that when he saw Mom reading stories to us on the lawn as he came home from work, he felt insecure and inadequate about how to love like that, so he would put the car in reverse and head to the bar for a drink.

But I never heard my father blame my mother for leaving, even as he struggled with various addictions. Even after he remarried, he told us over and over again, "Your mom was a good mother!"

Lesson Learned: Looking back on my parents' lives, I have learned that they had their own personal battles to fight even when I didn't understand them. Thanks be to God; He has been victorious in their lives!

Yes, I had a father wound, but I would not realize this until many years later. I loved him the best I knew how, but when I was young, I feared him more than I loved him. His firm discipline was amplified by the fact that he was 6' 5" tall! As I went through counseling I discovered how his strictness and mood swings influenced me, but when I was young, more often than not, I was simply scared and confused.

My father has come a long, long way from the man he was prior to 1979 to the man he is today. He celebrated 39 years of sobriety last month. He is an honest and humble man. I am proud of him for being honest enough to tell and own his story!

He even has a grateful attitude now about his own father's alcoholism. Five or six years into his sobriety, he told me that although he never heard his dad say I love you, he knew that his father loved him because of the effort he went to in very difficult times after World War 2 to put bread on the table. I deeply appreciate the attitude and perspective that my father has about his father, whom I am named after. And I agree with it very much.

However, I'm telling you the truth that I know how important it is to pray in order to gain and maintain such a grateful attitude, because I too had to change my attitude in order to love my father!!! It begins and ends with an attitude of surrender-surrendering feelings of anger and resentment, pride and entitlement. Those things are not necessarily accomplished overnight.

Lesson Learned: Looking back on the generations, I have learned that the sins of the family go forward "to the third and fourth generation of those who hate God, but God shows love to a thousand generations of those who love Him." Exodus 20:5-6

I became fascinated by sports early on, when my father would interrupt my sisters and me watching Saturday morning cartoons because he wanted to watch baseball, football, or golf on TV. Once, when I was little, I found a baseball bat in the basement which belonged to Dad, but I didn't know that until I got a spanking for hitting rocks with it in the backyard to our German Shepherd, Vic. I later learned that the bat was autographed by Alvin Dark. I think he played for the Oakland A's and was a highly respected baseball player at that time. He was later a manager in Major League Baseball.

As difficult as things were with my father, I also had some good times with him, such as on family camping outings or seeing him on water skis along with my mom. I have a very faint memory of my parents ice skating together. I remember him roller skating with us on his shoulders and I also remember him in the bowling alley! He loved a lot of different sports just like I did as I got older. His deepest love regarding sports was golf, as I would learn when we moved in with him and our stepmother in Louisiana as teenagers.

Lesson Learned: In looking back on my personal journey, it's important to acknowledge the truth about the hard times, but also to remember the times of great joy.

CHAPTER 5
Lessons of Pain

I had seven surgeries on my legs (mainly tendon releases) until I was roughly 13 or 14 years old. I don't remember my father coming to visit me in the hospital in the early years. After I lived with my mom and stepdad, I saw my stepdad at the hospital occasionally. However, my mom was there all the time!!!

Regarding my surgeries, I had a hard time lying still in the hospital, only to go home to lie in bed for a few more weeks. It was painful because my legs would spasm. My disability as well as my lot in life were far short of what I initially thought was good or fair. But this is a story of what God did and does in His magnificent love—to change the perspective of the ones He loves and magnify our understanding of how great He is. "And we know that in all things God works for the good of those who love him, who are called according to his purpose." Romans 8:28

Lesson Learned: Looking back on difficult times in my childhood, I have learned that God works things out for our good (even if we don't feel like it at the time).

When I was young, I was often anxious and felt like I had to be in control, i.e., to figure things out in my head first to see if they could be achieved or not. I would daydream and rehearse things in my mind. I rarely left room for spontaneity. I frequently tried to plan things out, weeks if not years ahead of time.

I was often filled with fear. When I went to the hospital, I was afraid I would die and wouldn't see my parents again. And I was afraid to die because I didn't know what would happen if you did! I guess I could have asked my mom or stepdad what happens when you die, but back then I remember thinking, "How would they know?" So I never bothered to ask.

I witnessed the deaths of John F. Kennedy, Bobby Kennedy, and Martin Luther King in close succession to one another on TV. This only made me more afraid. Mom put the painting of Jesus knocking at the door over the head of my bed after I was born, so when I was scared before going through my surgeries, she told me that Jesus would be with me.

There are a few occurrences of divine importance associated with my Heavenly Father and my earthly father. They are related to my hunger to fill the void in my life in unhealthy ways, while still seeing the hand of the Lord work along the way. My overwhelming sense of fear frequently affected my relationships with others, more so with men than with women. But when it came to transparency with women so that I could believe they cared for me? Yes, you bet that for lack of trust, I got scared! Fear had control of me.

I was afraid to let go of the control I thought I had. I had internal anger. When I was young and for many years into my adulthood, I was a perfectionist, and it is still a battle today at 60 years old.

Lesson Learned: Looking back on my fear, I have learned that God never lets go of our hand. Proverbs 3:5-6

Mom married Robert Harry Spalding in 1966. There were some good times with my stepdad, Harry. We would listen to him read *Bartholomew Cubbins and the 500 Hats* or *A Christmas Tale* with various accents. I remember making bets on football teams with him. Sometimes I would switch teams at halftime because my team was losing and I didn't want to lose out on ice cream. Sometimes he would get upset because he wanted me to understand the importance of a commitment. Sometimes he would let me switch teams and I would get ice cream. He did the best he could to suddenly be a father to three children without a lot of experience. He made sure there was food on the table. And he made sure that we went to church.

My mom and stepdad loved Colorado, including the University of Colorado Buffs, particularly quarterback Bobby Anderson because he went to Boulder High School. Mom was fond of the time she lived in Boulder, although she wasn't as fond of it after "the hippies came in and took over." She recalls the time (in Boulder) when her dad woke her up one night to go to the top of a mountain to see the fireworks go off in celebration of the end of World War II.

Lessons of Pain

My stepdad told me about baseball players named Carroll Hardy, Stan Musial, Babe Ruth, Lou Gehrig and others. And I fell in love with baseball after watching the movie, *Pride of the Yankees*. For a long time, baseball was the only girlfriend I ever really knew.

I loved sports movies because they gave me hope as a young boy! They showed me that athletes in different fields of sport might really care about young people like me! And they also encouraged me to consider being able to achieve great things of my own!

I still try to watch these movies once a year if not more.

Pride of the Yankees

The stars were Gary Cooper as Lou Gehrig, Teresa Wright as Lou Gehrig's wife, and Walter Brennan as the Yankee general manager. The real Babe Ruth played himself in the movie. What I remember about Lou Gehrig is that his parents came to America from Germany and his mom wanted Lou to become a lawyer and make good money because they were poor.

In one scene, Lou Gehrig's father told Lou that his mother was sick and in the hospital. He informed his son that he would like to put her in a private hospital where the best medicine was, so that she could heal. Upon hearing this, Lou decided on his own to drop out of Law School and then promptly signed a contract with the New York Yankees because the contract had enough money in it to help his mom.

From the very beginning it was obvious that Lou Gehrig had a loving and loyal affection for his mother, even though she thought baseball was just a game and a waste of time. I first thought that he was demonstrating a personal preference, but the action that he took was anything but a personal preference. It made me think of Romans 12 where it talks about offering your body as a Living Sacrifice. There is no mention of Jesus Christ in the movie but the action that Lou Gehrig took to help his mom spoke to me that way! His mom did get upset when he dropped out of Law School, because she thought baseball was nothing more than foolish child's play, yet she had no

17

idea why he really dropped out.

What I loved about Lou Gehrig was that he loved his mom! His mom was his first love!

He began to play baseball and after a while, both his mom and dad supported him. Then he met the love of his life at (where else?) but the baseball field.

As it turned out, signing on with the New York Yankees was the right choice for Lou Gehrig. He was regarded as the best first baseman in baseball when he died in 1941. He was the first New York Yankee to have his number retired, #4.

In the movie, some of the Yankee players went to visit children in the hospital. Babe Ruth was asked by a young boy if he would hit a homerun for him in the game later that afternoon. And Babe Ruth agreed. Then the same boy, when he met Lou Gehrig, asked, "Would you hit two home runs for me?" Kindly but astonished, Lou replied, "Boy oh Boy, you drive a hard bargain! But if I hit two home runs for you, I want you to do something for me. I want you to do your exercises and get well so that you can walk again!" The boy said OK, and they shook on it.

So Babe Ruth came up to bat when the Yankees played Chicago that afternoon. He pointed to left field and hit a homerun (where else?) but to left field! Then the announcer on the radio read a telegram that Babe Ruth had just hit a homerun for a young boy in the hospital.

Then Lou Gehrig stepped up to the plate and he too hit a homerun. The announcer said they had just received another telegram that Lou Gehrig had just hit a homerun for the same boy in the hospital that Babe Ruth had hit a homerun for! However, Lou Gehrig was not going to hit just one home run today, he was going to try to hit two for him!

And as you can imagine, all the fans listening to the game on the radio that day were on the edge of their seats!

Lessons of Pain

So Lou Gehrig made two more trips to the plate but no home run. Then he made one last trip to the plate. Radio announcer: "And he hit a long ball and it is gone!!! Lou Gehrig has just hit two home runs for a young boy in the hospital!!!" But the fans in the stands would not learn about this until they read the paper or heard it on the radio.

I always loved and believed this part of the movie was true, that both Babe Ruth and Lou Gehrig hit home runs for a boy in the hospital, but no one is sure if this really happened. I conclude that this was one of Hollywood's attempts to juice up the true facts of the movie.

In another scene, Mrs. Gehrig played a joke on Mr. Huggins, the Yankee General Manager and family friend. She told him she was convinced that Lou was seeing another girl. Mr. Huggins was very angry and said, "If this is true, I'll punch him in the nose myself! Friend or not." So the two of them drove to a small neighborhood ball field. And there was Lou Gehrig himself, umpiring for a little league team. At this, Mr. Huggins was angry and said, "You told me Lou was seeing another girl!"

At that moment. Mrs. Gehrig laughed! "He is!" she said. "Baseball is his other girl!"

Later on, she put together a horseshoe-shaped bouquet of roses to commemorate a special event the team held for Lou. When he got home, they greeted each other with kisses, lovingly collapsed on the floor, and playfully wrestled. For one brief moment at the end of this, Lou Gehrig experienced some pain in his shoulder. It was a signal of things to come.

Early the next season he was struggling to hit the ball. This continued for a few more games until they brought in a replacement. A few days later he went to the doctor for tests and when he returned for the results he said, "Give it to me straight, Doc! Am I going to die?" Reluctantly the doctor shook his head yes. And at that, he had a surprised look of sadness, confusion, and heartache on his face. Yet he mustered the strength to thank the doctor and say, "Do me a favor Doc. Don't tell my wife, okay?"

19

Later, Mrs. Gehrig paid a visit to the doctor herself. She convinced him to tell her. Briefly she cried in his arms but then said, "Don't tell Lou that I know."

On July 4, 1939, he went to the ballpark early. As he was making his way through the parking lot, he came across a handsome young man who asked, "Mr. Gehrig, do you remember me?"Lou looked and paused a moment but could not quite remember. "Well, I'm older now, but I'm the one you hit two home runs for a while back." And as you saw the look in Lou Gehrig's eyes, you could see that all of a sudden, he knew. He said congratulations and they spent a few moments together.

Then, in the movie, you saw Lou Gehrig in the tunnel in front of the stairs that lead to the field. As he approached the stairs, you could see Mrs. Gehrig in the background with a sad but encouraging look on her face as she stared at the #4 on the back of his jersey. But she stayed back in a loving way so that the moment could be his.

As he stood before the microphone to address the crowd, you could see the members of the two great Yankee teams he played for. One team stood in a row of bright white uniforms along the first-base line. And the other team stood the same way along the third-base line. Then he began to speak those famous words.

"I am the luckiest man on the face of the Earth. I got a bad break, but I've got an awful lot to live for!"

You can faintly hear his speech continue while some other remarks are made about Lou on the film. But now it is the audience's turn to see the back of his jersey for a final time as he disappears down the stairs toward the locker room. And the screen fades to black. The End.

Lesson Learned: Looking back at movies about people I admire, I have learned to emulate positive qualities in others. Many of those qualities were achieved through pain and suffering. It's important to learn the lessons. Their suffering was not in vain!

CHAPTER 6
Lessons of Patience

When my sisters and I spent time with our dad (after my parents divorced but before Dad married again), we frequently had to spend the night in the car while Dad worked at the Red Owl Grocery Store stocking shelves as a second job. He could not afford a babysitter. My sisters would take turns pushing their feet up against the front passenger seat where I sat. They bounced my body and we all laughed!

It seemed like that was the way we would always begin things together while we were in the parking lot in that old car, but we would soon grow tired of the bouncing game and start picking at the stuffing in the ceiling of the car. The first few times we did it, we only did it a little bit because we were afraid we might get in trouble. But one particular night, we got carried away until there was stuffing all around the car and all over us and Dad got so mad! We all got a terrible spanking and cried all the way home!

Years later, after Dad got sober, he told me that when he got mad that night he took it out on us, but he was really mad at himself because he realized it was unfair to expect three young children under the age of 10 to spend the night in the car and not get bored to death!

Not long after the incident in the car, he took us to Calvary Temple Church. It was near the time of my birthday. I remember this because they sang "Happy Birthday" to me in children's Sunday School. We also sang "Jesus loves me this I know for the Bible tells me so!" This song even today resonates in my spirit as you will see. It felt so good to sing "Jesus loves me" because I missed my mom so much.

As we were leaving the church and were in the parking lot, Dad spoke to a church pastor or an elder (I don't quite remember which). He told the man, "I am an alcoholic and I need help." The man replied, "Come back when you decide you want to get sober." But what he did not understand was that Dad was sober that day. Yes, there were many days that he was not sober, that is, until he got sober for good in 1979. But on that particular day in the early to mid-1960's, he was sober!

Dad once told me a story of manipulating circumstances to get your way. It shows how sins travel forward to the third and fourth generation. The story goes that when he was in school, he asked the playground supervisor if he and his buddies could use the playground with the basketball court so they could play basketball. The supervisor replied, "I don't know. You'll have to ask the girls (that were playing there). And if they're not willing to go elsewhere, you and your friends will have to find some other game to play."

So instead of asking the girls (because Dad knew there was a good chance they would say no), he went into a field not far from the playground and got a bull snake and put it in a coffee can. Then he dumped the snake onto the playground and scared the girls away. So my dad and the boys had the playground to themselves!

(The apple doesn't fall far from the tree! Haha!)

Lesson Learned: Looking back on Dad's life, I have learned that God gives us a lifetime to grow in wisdom toward Him to make necessary changes.

Dad married my stepmom, Shirley, in 1965, and together we went sledding and bowling and roller skating and did some of the things that we used to do when my mom and dad were married. During this time, I remember the 1965 flood of the Platte River. We were at Grandma's house and could not get back home until the next day. But the three of us children were only with Dad and Shirley for about a year. Then we went to live with Mom and our stepfather, Harry.

Dad and Shirley are still married to this day but have no children together. Mom and Harry had two sons. Robert, my half-brother, was born in 1968 so he is ten years younger than me. We watched Sesame Street together and Robert loved to make a scary Cookie Monster face, although Cookie Monster was anything but scary. My mom took care of a little girl and she loved Robert. Mom would give her a cookie, but she would always ask for another for Robert. We tell Robert that she was his first girlfriend.

My little brother, Teddy, was born in 1971. He was like Linus in the *Peanuts* cartoon, always walking around with his cute little face, a blanket, and two middle fingers in his mouth.

Lesson Learned: God has a purpose for family, even if it means having more than one mom and dad!

I started going to the Easter Seals Handicamp in Idaho Springs, Colorado in the mid 60's. We always checked into camp on Saturday mornings and Mom gave me a hug and kiss and said goodbye. She would pick me up two weeks later.

(By the way, in the mid-60's, I was an Easter Seals poster child.)

I want to take a moment to say thank you to the Lord and to some very special people related to the Easter Seals Handicamp. Some paid our way as sponsors so we could attend the camp when our parents could not afford it. Some were the physical therapists and financial providers at Sewell Rehabilitation who assisted me, Victor, Charlie, Joe, and so many other children like us. I went there for therapy to make my legs stronger.

One of the last times I would see my father for a long time was when he brought a brand new fishing rod to me before I went to

Handicamp. He spent some time with me and then he hugged me and said goodbye. I did not know then, but I would not see him again for nine years.

The first time I went fishing at Handicamp I thought of my dad and felt so alone! There was an ache deep inside that haunted me for many years to come.

The camp counselors would come over and cast our fishing rods with a line, bobber, hook and bait. I remember not knowing how important it was to keep your line in the water, so I would reel my line in and scream for help to put it back on the water again. Sometimes they would get frustrated with me because I seemed more interested in watching my bobber race back in toward me. And then the counselor would say firmly, "Now leave it out there!"

The fact that he yelled at me triggered memories of my father. I was holding the rod he gave me but now felt the lonely ache inside, so I looked out at a small mountain with a gold-colored patch as if it were a bald spot on a man's head. I prayed to God in my pain and asked Him, "God, if you are real, would you please show yourself to me?"

I am grateful to Jesus that He heard my cry and eventually answered me, in 1979. I know there was a god-shaped vacuum inside my soul where the Holy Spirit belongs, but because I was so young, I did not understand this at the time.

There is a song we sang before every meal at Handicamp that I remember very well. It is the Johnny Appleseed song and it goes like this:

"Oh the Lord is good to me, and so I thank the Lord,
for giving me the things I need,
the sun and the rain and the apple seed,
Oh the Lord is good to me."

You might remember the story in the Bible about how faith grows like a mustard seed. A mustard seed is one of the smallest seeds that can be planted. However, it grows to become one of the tallest plants. So maybe God was cultivating and growing the apple seed so I would have the strength and courage to continue to pray the questions I had…and so that my faith would grow. But at the time, I wondered if anybody heard me or cared.

Here is a line from a song by an old favorite rock and roll band named Chicago. "Does anybody really know what time it is? Does anybody really care?" I sang this in my heart, but as you will see, God didn't choose to answer my cry when I was nine years old.

Lesson Learned: God has a way of sowing sovereign seeds into our lives, but sometimes they don't bloom until later.

CHAPTER 7
Lessons of Childhood

I attended two special education schools in the Denver area (the equivalent of elementary plus middle school in public school language). The first was Fletcher Miller School. I went there for grades one and two, through the first year of my dad's marriage to Shirley.

I moved to Boettcher Elementary School for disabled children for third and fourth grades. My sisters and I were then living with my mom and stepdad. Boettcher was very close to the original Children's Hospital located at 20th and Downing. It was so close that there was an underground tunnel where many of the students who needed physical therapy would go to get their therapy.

My teacher was Mrs. M. She constantly asked us what time we had gone to bed the night before (if she caught us yawning in class). If we were caught yawning, it was like sticking a coin into a machine to hear a recorded message! She would tell us to go to bed at 8 p.m. because we needed eight hours of sleep in order to function well in the classroom each day. And if we were whispering to one of our classmates instead of doing our work, she would pull her glasses down to the end of her nose and look at us over the top of them until she heard adequate silence! It seemed like she was always picking on me (I wonder why!), but she had good reason because I had attention span issues and I loved to talk if I got bored.

My misfortune was that I had to take my third-grade subjects in her fourth-grade classroom, so I had Mrs. M. for two consecutive years. She did a good job as a teacher because everyone learned and nobody stepped too far out of line. But almost everyone was bored because her personality was dry and she would nag about her pet peeves a lot!

I don't remember my fifth-grade teacher's name because I wasn't there long, but she was so nice. While there, I was friends with Joe L. and Victor M.

Lesson Learned: We don't always get to choose who our teachers are! Haha!

Then we moved to Lakewood. I went to school at Fletcher Miller again where most of my classes were with Mrs. W. We took tests at the start of the year (and the end of the year) to find out what we could remember about what we had learned. There was a lot of overlap so it always seemed like we were studying things I thought I was finished with.

We played a lot of games in Mrs. W's classroom. For example, she encouraged the students to study math by throwing a rubber ball with suction cups at the chalkboard. She made targets with different numbers on the board. We would make two or three throws and then add the numbers together if we were doing addition. Same with subtraction, multiplication, division, and fractions.

I don't remember ever studying American History or Science at Fletcher Miller except through little booklets called SRA.

Then there was Spelling, which we always did on Thursdays and Fridays. Charts were kept on the wall to indicate our scores. If you missed a word on your spelling test on Thursday, you had a chance to take it again on Friday. If you missed a word or words on Friday, the red line would drop accordingly. I remember doing pretty well in Spelling, but one year I misspelled one word all year long. I was so frustrated because there were so many perfect scores that year. The next year, my last year, I did not misspell a single word all year. I was very competitive about everything I did at Fletcher Miller.

I was competitive in swimming class. I was competitive in gym class when we ran or competed in various sports. I was competitive in music class when remembering names of musical instruments (or rock and roll artists on Fridays). I was competitive in art class to try and make the best bowl or animal figure from clay.

One year, the students had a chance to compete against other disabled students from around the US to create a piece of Christmas art. I went home and talked to Mom about how to draw the twelve drummers drumming. She taught me how to draw one English soldier and then how to trace the outside from the top of his black fluffy hat down to his shoes, eleven more times. She showed me how to do this because I was frustrated that I didn't know how to draw a line of English soldiers and I wanted to win. I followed Mom's verbal description on a sheet of paper for practice and she said, "Honey, that's great!!! Good job!!!"

I trusted my mom because she's a talented artist! When I heard the tone of her voice, I knew I had done exactly what she had described, so I drew him for real with a black hat and a red coat and white criss-cross straps with a drum at his waist and white gloves and drumsticks. Then I shadowed the single soldier with eleven consecutive lines beside him totaling twelve drummers drumming! Before Christmas, I discovered that my depiction had been chosen for the *Twelve Days of Christmas* picture book! (There were twelve winners to represent each of the twelve Days of Christmas.)

Lesson Learned: Listen to the wisdom of others.

CHAPTER 8
Lessons of Disappointment

When I was about 13, I met a counselor at Easter Seals Handicamp named Carol. She was my first crush! That year, the camp counselors put together a Dating Game like we used to watch on television. They asked me if I would participate. I told them I would not participate unless Carol was included. They replied, "Come on now! You know we can't do it that way!" So I said, "Okay, then I'm not playing the game." Twice more they asked me, and I gave the same answer, so finally they said, "Okay, we'll see what we can do."

They tried to trick me by asking Carol to disguise her voice, but I caught on right away and just played along. I asked each female counselor or camper that was included as a prospective date a question and when I recognized Carol's voice, I pretended like I didn't recognize it. I asked all my other questions to the other ladies. And when it came time to choose my date, I chose Carol because I knew who she was from the beginning.

I frequently knew when I was growing up what I wanted, so I manipulated circumstances to try and get my way! (This reminds me of my dad manipulating circumstances with the bull snake.) I wanted Carol and I got Carol. They told us we had to choose if we wanted an ice cream date or a swim in the pool date. I did not tell them I wanted both, so I chose the pool date. She was beautiful! She was so sweet!

We swam in the warm water and she even held me in her arms! Wow! I felt as though I was in heaven! I then asked her if she would get ice cream! She did, and we finished our ice cream in the pool. I got both!

Then I asked her to get me a Baby Ruth bar and she did. She broke out laughing when she saw what I did with it next. I saw some kids swimming at the other end of the pool and I wanted the pool to ourselves just like we had had when we first got in.

So, I unwrapped the candy bar and threw it all the way down to the other end. The kids thought somebody went to the bathroom in the pool, so they screamed and got out of the pool. And I didn't say a word. I just laughed! And so did she, but then she said to me with a smile in her eyes, "Randy, that wasn't very nice." I said, "I know. I won't do it again."

I told you the apple doesn't fall far from the tree!

Lesson Learned: We need to learn to play along and coexist with others, and not always demand that there be changes.

For the next few days after the Dating Game, I always wanted to be around Carol. She made me smile inside. The ache I often felt inside, for now, was gone.

On the last day we were there, I knew she was going back home to another state. The closer the time came for my mom to pick me up, the ache started returning. As she gave me a kiss on the cheek and said goodbye, I started to cry! And I cried off and on throughout the weekend after I returned home.

From this time forward every time I met a lady I really liked I was glad, but I would cry as soon as I had to go home. The ache of loneliness would hover over me like a deep, dark cloud. That ache would soon begin to haunt me in various other ways, such as when I got yelled at because my chores weren't done or done correctly...or even when I didn't perform in my athletic endeavors to meet my own expectations. I felt the cloud hanging over me again and again, just like when Charlie Brown would throw a pitch and crack!!! Here came the baseball right back at him only to knock him down. And for a very brief instant, you would see Charlie Brown sitting on top of the mound in his underwear. And before the next pitch would come, you would see him standing erect on the mound again, talking to himself in an attempt to correct the situation in his mind. But he would throw the next pitch only to see the exact same thing happen again! And again! And again. And sometimes after a few pitches and more of the same results, a dark black rain cloud would empty itself nowhere but right on top of his head.

Likewise, when you would hear the muffled sound of a horn symbolizing the voice of the teacher, all of a sudden, gloom or despair would appear on Charlie Brown's face. I often identified with and felt like poor Charlie Brown!!!

Lesson Learned: Sometimes it is just that way in life. It's like waves that roll onto the shore. If you build a sandcastle close to the water's edge and leave it there, you'll find that the break of a new day has washed it away.

CHAPTER 9
Lessons of Perseverance

One Halloween, Mom said I was too old to trick-or-treat so I talked my youngest brother, Teddy, into taking an extra trick-or-treat sack with him for his sick brother, because, oh man, do I love candy! I told Teddy I would give him half. That's probably why he lost all his teeth, haha! No, that's really because of a bicycle accident, or subsequent rugby or football injury when he was at Kennedy High School.

Teddy and I had an awful lot in common when it came to sports. I taught him how to throw a football and he taught me how to laugh at life! We had many conversations about God and politics. We both loved Ronald Reagan, Bill McCartney, the Colorado Buffaloes, and last but not least, the Denver Broncos. How could anybody not love the Denver Broncos, haha!

When I was in my mid-teens, I tried to teach Teddy to defend himself against the older and bigger neighborhood bullies. I found a way to get even with them, even though I was on crutches, and they did not bother my brother again. No one was going to mess with my little brother! I did my best to look after my younger sisters and brothers.

Brenda, Lana, Robert, and Teddy (my siblings) and I had our disagreements from time to time, like all siblings do, but nobody from the outside was going to disturb the bond of love we had, and have, for each other.

Lesson Learned: True love means going to the end to defend and protect.

I do want to say that later in life, I have had many conversations with all my family about Jesus and what the scriptures say about sanctification, suffering for the sake of Jesus, and so on.

As I have said, I've always liked movies about athletes. One of my other favorites was the 1970's made-for-tv movie *Brian's Song*. This was about the lives of two rookie football players trying to make the Chicago Bears football team. Both made the team and the coach asked them to be roommates. This is significant because Gale Sayers was a black running back from the University of Kansas and Brian Piccolo was a white running back from Wake Forest University in North Carolina.

What stood out to me was not just that this was the first time that a black and a white football player would room together, but that they pushed each other to be better and became very close friends.

At one point when Gale Sayers got hurt, Brian Piccolo encouraged him to get stronger through his recovery. Soon they were playing side by side in the backfield again. Then Brian began to slow down as a player, and the two roommates, who were now like brothers, learned that Brian had cancer. Gale stayed with him until his last breath from lung cancer.

Another sports movie I loved was called *Radio*. I also loved World War II movies. As you know, I love stories that uncover the importance of perseverance and the significance of a group of people coming together to help each other heal and overcome the wounds and mistakes of the past. Together.

Lesson Learned: You don't just play for yourself and you don't just live for yourself! You play for each other and you live for each other! This became more and more emphasized as I began my walk with Jesus Christ.

Around this time, my godparents gave me a snow cone machine, so I decided to make a business out of it. My sister, Brenda, and I set up a Snow Cone stand near the local drug store. (Brenda was my business manager.) After the snow cone syrup ran out, we turned it into a Kool-Aid stand. It was hard to buy new snow cone syrup, but Kool-Aid was easy to acquire at the drug store. (Side note: After a while, the owner of the drug store got a little upset because he thought we were affecting his beer sales. The Pepsi delivery man overheard this conversation and donated a case of Pepsi to us to sell!)

Lessons of Perseverance

Once, while Brenda was inside making more Kool-Aid, a boy who Brenda recognized from Robert W. Steele School, came up and stole our money can. Brenda chased him home, told his mother what had happened, then went to get help from a neighbor detective, Mr. Larson, who was also a Kool-Aid patron. With his help the money was returned, and in addition, the mother told her son he needed to pay a quarter for every dollar in the can, so he did! The can had $32 in it, so that was a lot of money for the boy to pay. As it turned out, not only did we get our money back, but we made money on the deal! We called it the Great Kool-Aid Stand Robbery. Mr. Larson had his hand in getting our story on the second page of The Denver Post!

Lesson Learned: God has a way of making people pay!

FROM HIS STAND AT S. VIRGINIA AVE. AND S. VINE ST., RANDY MILLIKEN OFFERS A PASSERBY A SOFT DRINK
With him are, from left, his sisters, Brenda, 9, and Lana, 8, and Ernest M. Larson, who called police to his aid.

Business Back to Normal After Con Raid

By PAT McGRAW

Business is back to usual now, thank you, for a small-town Denver small businessman.

He was the victim Sunday of a loss of funds, but the police got him his money back.

Randy Milliken, 11, a cheerful price victim, said the sum was R.D. Randy is the proprietor of a soft-drink stand at the corner of E. Virginia Ave. and S. Vine St.

Randy, son of Mr. and Mrs. Harry Spalding, 677 S. Vine St., said the incident occurred when two "big boys" and two "little ones" distracted him late Sunday afternoon while he was on the job.

A member of the group asked if he could count the money Randy's enterprise had taken in.

"A little girl told me they took some, though," Randy said.

The Boettcher Elementary school fifth grader said he told the group to empty their pockets, which they did, but Randy noticed one had not turned out his back pocket.

The attention of the police was brought to the case when Ernest M. Larson, a salesman for John K. Reed Realty, overheard Randy talking about the incident Monday. Reed

Realty is on the same corner as Randy's enterprise.

Larson said the report "made me hopping mad, and I called the police."

Patrolman Louis VomMarsall responded. He said he got Randy's money back for him and notified the parents of those involved.

Randy and his sisters, Brenda, 9, assistant manager of the firm, and Lana, 8, employee, hypothesize that the incident was to acquire funds to establish a competing soft-drink stand.

Randy's business, according to assistant manager Brenda, has been plagued with bad weather but still has managed to clear 50 cents to $1 a day. The money garnered from the firm's 15 a.m. until 6 p.m. efforts are used to finance trips to the movies.

Raw materials are purchased from a nearby drugstore with funds from the stand; ice is supplied two or three times a day from the family refrigerator—which is hard on the evening martini, according to Mrs. Spalding.

A proprietor of a snow cone stand until his snow cone machine broke, Randy expects to continue with the soft-drink business for the rest of the summer.

One day in the early 70's, I talked to my friend Jim about wheelchair basketball while on the school bus. He gave me two tickets to one of his games. My stepdad said he and I could go. I waited with eager anticipation for him to get home! I went into the back alley to shoot hoops with a little rubber ball. My sisters were playing somewhere close by. My little sister Lana tried to make a quick break for the bathroom and fell. A car that she didn't see ran over her ankle. Don't get me wrong, it was sad to see what happened to my little sister, but I was eager to see the wheelchair basketball game because I wanted to see if it was something I might be able to play. I was anxious for years because I didn't get to see that game.

During this time, I often told my Fletcher teachers that I was going to play professional sports. I don't doubt ever saying this since I had fantasized about being on a professional baseball, football, or basketball team for years. When I was in my bedroom, listening to the radio, or daydreaming at school, I would try anything to escape the reality of living with cerebral palsy in my youth.

I was definitely in denial about my disability growing up! I was also in denial through my effort to find and date able-bodied girls/women as I grew up. The choices I made are my responsibility beyond a shadow of a doubt, but I was also confused. While my father was in the middle of his addiction issues, he would encourage me to keep my mind off my disability and keep up with my sisters, or I was going to get a spanking! But during parent-teacher conferences, my teachers would encourage my mom to work with me at facing reality regarding my physical limitations.

Concerning wheelchair basketball, several of my teachers put me in a wheelchair and raced up and down the court past me. They were trying to tell me that my eye-hand coordination would not be good enough to compete alongside paraplegics in wheelchair basketball. I told them I didn't care how hard they tried to humiliate me on the court, I was going to play wheelchair basketball!

Later, Fletcher Miller School put on a student-teacher softball game and I told them I was going to play softball someday like them. Again, they put me on the field and tried to show me that I didn't have the coordination to play fastpitch softball because I couldn't catch and I couldn't hit! But I told them again, "I don't care how much you guys frustrate me or humiliate me, I'm going to play softball someday!"

And during this same period, several of my friends at Fletcher Miller started three soccer teams. Two of them would play on one asphalt field for two days. One day we would play the first half of the game and the second day we would play the second half during lunch recess. It would take two days to play one game. The other team would practice against each other for two days on the tetherball court while the other team was playing. These games went on all year.

We brought all three teams together to make one solid team when we played the Denver Kickers amateur soccer team by placing the Kickers in wheelchairs. The Fletcher Miller combined team beat the Denver Kickers 14 — 2. During the game, I started as Goalie for the first half and then played Halfback and Forward during the second half.

The gym teacher helped us put the big game together. She told us that the person who sold the most tickets to the game (which would take place at Lakewood High School) would win an authentic soccer ball. I went all around my neighborhood and sold tickets for $1 each. Some of the people I sold tickets to were elderly and couldn't go to the game. They told me to give the ticket to somebody who wanted to go but couldn't afford a ticket. I never actually found anyone like that, but I didn't try to either. I regret that, but I sold 150 tickets to the game and won the soccer ball.

Near the end of my time at Fletcher Miller, I was able to participate in Special Olympics competitions. I made State twice. I won a Silver in the softball throw, which included competition against able-bodied students. I won a Bronze in the 50-yard dash and another Bronze in the 440 relay. We tagged each other's crutches for the relay! I fondly remember two of my fellow player/coaches, Curt G. and Jim H.

CHAPTER 10
Lessons of Self-Awareness

A good friend at Fletcher Miller was Cliff. A couple of times, I was able to spend time with him at his home in the mountains of Berthoud, Colorado. At my house on Saturday mornings, I would watch Saturday morning cartoons, but things were different at Cliff's house. There, even if you were a guest, you participated in Saturday morning chores before anyone could watch TV, like helping to clean the house or making homemade butter. Even that was fun because his mom and dad helped you feel good about yourself as you helped around the house.

One day, the two of us started talking to our teacher, Mrs. W., about horses. Since Cliff lived the country farm life, he knew a lot more about horses than I did. We both knew that our teacher owned quarter horses that she and her husband raced at Santa Anita Horse Track in California and a few other places. We asked if she could show us how horse track betting worked. We were too young to bet legally at Centennial Race Track in Colorado so she gave each of us a roll of dimes. She taught us to observe several things about the horse and jockey, such as the track conditions, when a particular horse won, what kind of track the horse preferred when he won—wet or dry (same with the jockey), and how well the horse performed in previous races (same with the jockey). Did the horse win several times in a row? Did the jockey win several times in a row? Had the jockey ridden the horse he was on anytime recently?

We would make decisions about which horse we thought would win and there were 10 to 11 races on a card. Our teacher would tell us who scored the best at the end of the day.

The next spring, I told my stepfather's father (my Grandpa Spalding) that I knew how to bet on horses and win. He didn't believe me, but he challenged me! He asked me to decide who I thought the winning horse would be in a certain race, then gave money to my teacher so she could place the bet legally.

I looked at a horse, the performance records of the jockey and horse, and at the condition of the track. I noticed that the jockey had ridden this horse before, successfully! I was confident that this horse could win but I wanted to play it safe since I was playing with my step-grandfather's money. The book said the horse liked to come from behind. The odds on this horse winning this particular race were 12 to 1. I don't remember exactly how much money my grandfather gave me to give to the teacher. All I know is that it was a sizable amount.

One of the things I learned was that if you placed the bet so the horse shows (meaning it finishes first, second, or third) and you bet the horse to show, you won third-place money. The horse came from behind just like the book said and won the race, but I had placed money on him to show, so I got third place money. My step-grandfather, to say the least, was very surprised! He was also proud of me for being safe with his money and betting on the horse to show. He said I was wise and said, "Good job!" Then he gave me half of the winnings! It was somewhere over $100, which was great because I never expected to get any of it.

Lesson Learned: It was the only horse race in my life to this day that was bet on at the window, and I won. It was 1973 and I was 15 years old. I won my fair share of races with the dimes our teacher gave to Cliff and me, but as I learned about my competitive nature along with my addictive personality, I was always scared to go back to the race track! I praise the Lord for the awareness he has given to me on issues like this over the years.

CHAPTER 11
Lessons of Adolescence

When the time came for high school, there was talk about disabled students being mainstreamed into area high schools. I was close to many of the people I played soccer with and they were being considered for mainstreaming. Because I was competitive, I did not want to be left behind.

Again, my teachers started talking to me about not accepting reality. They said, "Randy, not everyone is capable of handling the pressure that goes along with being mainstreamed into public school. Some of these students who are being chosen may not make it either. You are not smart enough or emotionally stable enough to handle this!"

I asked for extra credit work to show them I could handle it, but that work didn't help me, which was partly my fault. I tried to keep up with all my favorite sports teams on the radio first. The games would end around 10 p.m. so I was already pretty tired by then. Then I would start working on my homework until 1:00 a.m.

I didn't know about boundaries needed to keep the most important priorities first, so when I turned in my extra credit work, a lot of my answers were wrong. This only validated and consolidated my teachers' and parents' views as to whether I could handle responsibilities in a public high school where students might be made fun of if they couldn't keep up.

I thought my chance to try my hand at public high school had gone by the wayside.

But as I look back, I can certainly see the hand of the Sovereign Lord and how He was involved even before I acknowledged Him as my Savior and Lord. It was He who allowed me to be born with cerebral palsy because He wanted to use it for His glory! And it was He who heard me ask in 1967 at the fishing pond at Easter Seals Handicamp, "God, if you are real, would you please show yourself to me?"

He did exactly that in the summer of 1979. And He also opened up the opportunity for me to attend a regular high school.

Lessons Learned from the Bottom of the Stairs

It began like this. During the nine years I didn't see my father, I spent a lot of time watching baseball, college basketball, and professional football on TV. If I saw Louisiana State University or Ole Miss football or basketball, it made me wonder about my father because I knew he and my stepmother lived in nearby Baton Rouge. When the LSU Tigers played the #3 University of Colorado in 1971, I wondered if Dad was thinking about me and my sisters. The Colorado Buffs had two quarterbacks from Louisiana in 1971, David Williams and Clyde Crutchmer, which, of course, also made me think of my dad. Colorado finished #3 behind Nebraska and Oklahoma that year.

I frequently lived vicariously through the athletes I watched on TV. One was Pistol Pete Maravich, who played basketball for the LSU Tigers and later with the New Orleans Jazz of the NBA. (David Thompson was my favorite player in Denver. He played at the same time Pistol Pete did.) I associated sports with life. It made geography come to life! And it simply made me feel closer to my dad. (My dad also loved Fords, Chevrolets, and Volkswagens. If I saw these cars on the road it would remind me of him. And I wondered if he was thinking about me.)

By this time, my sisters and I were in our teenage years. This was hard on our mom because we were going through rebellion or at least thinking we knew more about life than Mom or our stepfather did. So Mom made arrangements through my Aunts Carolyn and Bobby (who were on my father's side of the family) so we could see our father again. I think she was hoping it might relieve some of the tension that she and we were experiencing.

She had one important stipulation. If we were going to see our father, she did not want any secrets. She simply wanted to know if he was in town. One night, he showed up without advance notification and it made her upset and the next thing we knew, the three of us were at Aunt Carolyn's house on our way to Baton Rouge.

I was particularly interested in going simply because my father told me they did not have special education schools there and it was my dream to have a chance to go to a regular school.

My mom called Aunt Carolyn to talk to us about the previous night. I told her I loved her very much and did not have anger or hard feelings. I simply wanted a chance to go to a regular school. She understood and we were on our way to a new and different life in Louisiana.

Because of the traditional high school background my sister Brenda had, she started as a junior at Tara High School in Louisiana in mid-1976. I worked out details to graduate early with the class of '78, so I started off two weeks later than Brenda as a sophomore in 1976. Lana started off at Westdale Junior High in '76, then one year later joined us at Tara. In 1977, Brenda was a senior, I was a junior, and Lana was a sophomore.

CHAPTER 12
Lessons of Teamwork

I tried to sign up as a team manager for the three major sports teams at Tara. I was accepted as a manager for both basketball and baseball and it remained that way until I graduated in 1978.

On my first day as a basketball team manager, after the game, our coach Bill W. was celebrating his birthday in the locker room. His wife brought in a birthday cake and I asked what flavor it was. Coach said, "It's German Chocolate. Want some?" And almost immediately I began to feel accepted by my coach and the players. To this day, my favorite cake is German Chocolate.

When football started, we had pep rallies in the gym on game days (Fridays). This was an invigorating experience for me. It would start off early in the morning and the cheerleaders would bring favors of candy and encouragement notes to the athletes and the members of the team. And yes, that included team managers!

The pep rallies usually only took place during football season. Still it was so beautiful! The teachers, principals, front office, and all the students packed the stands. Whoever wanted to speak would just get up and give a word of encouragement that was intended not just for the football players, but for the entire student body. Players shared memories and motivational thoughts. The band played the school song and other motivational songs with rhythms and cadences to motivate the fans for a game that was only a few hours away! Cheerleaders and flag girls shared their talents. Students wrote and shared inspirational stories and poems.

(By the way, in my senior year, I asked my sister, Brenda, to be my homecoming date! It was a memorable night.)

I was learning on the fly how to write poems, but it wasn't hard because my father frequently played rock and roll music around the house and lines from the songs in the 60's and 70's inspired me to think about how I felt inside. So I started writing poems for the pep rallies. We often had a theme associated with that week's opponent, so I would dress according to the theme and compose poetry. If the theme was "Sock it to the Panthers," I would pin socks to my ankles and socks to my knees and socks to my bottom and socks to my sleeves and then write a poem titled "Sock it to the Panthers!" I did this for every single pep rally until I graduated. I was nominated for Most School Spirit as a junior, but juniors weren't eligible, so I didn't win, but I won as a senior!

I took a lot of public speaking classes at the advice of the guidance counselors because they noticed that I often looked down at my shoes when addressing them. But for some reason, I didn't have that problem when it came to talking about sports!

One comment before I move on. When I became a Christian and begin to follow Jesus Christ, I learned early on the importance of community and unity! As I write this, I'm realizing that my first experience with community and unity was while I was a student at Tara. I felt it in the Commons area—a carpeted area where all the students would gather before the class day started and certainly during the pep rallies. I even felt it in the classrooms, which was very different for me compared to my school experiences just a few months back in Denver.

One day, I was fooling around with David H., one of the basketball team members, just as practice was getting started. We were arm wrestling and the Coach W. blew the whistle. For an instant I thought I was in trouble but quickly Coach said, "If Randy wins this match, every one of you will be on the line to run ladders!"

I was sad when I won...for a moment! But my teammates were good sports. They were amazed at the physical strength I had!

Around this time, my stepmom and dad went on vacation and gave us instructions not to drive Dad's truck except for grocery shopping. But one of my sister's friends told us a story about a mythical monster on a nearby lake, so we all climbed into the truck to see if we could see it. We didn't see a thing. To make matters worse, the next-door neighbor saw us climb into the truck. It was past 10 p.m. when we did it, so she told our parents when they got home. We were grounded for the rest of the semester. That meant I wouldn't be able to perform my duties as a team manager because I couldn't attend that semester's games. I really wanted to earn a high school letter jacket and I was looking forward to it.

Also, we couldn't leave the house early for school, so that meant I wouldn't be able to fulfill my duties as a Senior Senator. My friend, Lyn, had told me that they gave out awards for high marks of achievement in student government.

I was so disappointed, but I had a plan! I would tell Coach the truth and hope that if I admitted I was wrong, he could find a way for me to get extra credit work so I could still earn my letter jacket. And if Lyn could swing by my house on her way to school and pick me up, but not arrive until 9:00 sharp, I could make it to the student government meetings in time. I told Lyn, "You watch! I'm going to win that high achievement award!" And I did, even though I was grounded.

I deserved to be grounded because I was wrong to violate the rules my parents had set. Yet I still won a plaque for outstanding Senior Senator!

My dad lectured me on the way to the spring sports award banquet that maybe next time I could win a letter jacket if I obeyed my parents. I listened but didn't say a word back. I only hoped there was a surprise in store for both of us!

I sat at the banquet with Dad and my baseball and basketball teammates. They started to hand out the awards for basketball. All my teammates and fellow team managers got letter jackets and awards! I started to sigh, thinking the one thing I wanted to earn the most had gotten away!

But then Coach W. shouted out, "Would Randy Milliken please come forward?" I did, and he asked me to turn my back to him and face the crowd. (Tears are coming from my eyes even now as I write this.) My basketball teammates, coach, and two other team managers draped a burgundy red wool letter jacket with gold stripes on the cuffs and a big gold T on the front over my shoulders as I was crying! And I got a standing ovation.

I remember asking the coach when this whole extra credit thing had started! He had never said yes. He had never said no. He had only said he would see what he could do. But when he asked me if I was wrong to do what I did, I said, "Yes! I'm sorry, please forgive me!" He thanked me for being honest. Looking back now, even though I had not yet accepted Jesus as my Savior or acknowledged him as my Lord, I know He was behind it.

On the way home, Dad was as surprised as I was! He asked, "How did you bleep bleep get that letter jacket? I thought you told me you wouldn't be able to get it." I said, "It's true, I did tell you that. But what I did not tell you was that I asked Coach W. for extra credit work and told him that I was wrong to do what I did." And my dad replied in a calm voice, "Son, you just don't give up when you want something bad enough, do you?" I said, "No, I don't, and I learned it from you! Dad, I'm sorry I didn't listen to you. I want to say the same thing to you that I said to the coach. Please forgive me. I love you and I was not trying to get this letter jacket to stick it in your face. Sometimes I'm confused about your feelings for me. Sometimes I even get really angry because you can be really hard to deal with! I don't know why that is, but I do love you!"

That was the last time I was able to be really honest with my father until after he got sober.

Lesson Learned: "Above all, keep fervent in your love for one another, because love covers a multitude of sins." 1 Peter 4:8

Later, the baseball team was preparing to host the annual Tara High Easter baseball tournament. Coach M. was not happy with the way our team had practiced prior to the tournament, so when the players came to the dugout after practice he yelled out, "I'm not happy with this practice. Every one of you is going to run the bases!"

After all the players exited the dugout, Coach M. turned to me and said, "Did you hear me?! That means you too!" With excitement I asked, "Can I slide when I reach home?" He said, "Yes. Get out there!" All the players had reached home plate by the time I was crossing first and they were cheering for me as I rounded third and headed for home. When I slid I let out a yell of excitement! Then my teammates picked me up and set me back on my feet.

We won that Easter baseball tournament. My teammates seemed to be energized when I chose to slide into home with my crutches!

I didn't get a letter on my jacket for baseball but my teammates gave me something I still have today—a baseball autographed by the whole team! I lost my letter jacket when I got older in the process of moving. And I don't know where my Senior Senator award is, but my autographed baseball stands alongside hundreds of others, most of which have Bible verses on them from sharing my faith with baseball players!

These baseballs are now placed on shelves which are literally over my bed. My friends, Cliff Stein, Mike McClure, Tim McClure (not related), Danny Wood and Dan Sauvageau helped my collection grow from 60 to over 450!

Lesson Learned: Even though I treasure this collection, Jesus Christ is higher and more deserving of our time and worship than anything we may have. Do not worship the created thing. Worship the Creator! And one more thing. You're always "safe at home plate" with Jesus!
John 3:16

CHAPTER 13
Lessons of Persistence

When I started attending Tara, my homeroom class was the American History classroom with Steve M., who was also the baseball coach. He was a great teacher, whether he was teaching about Thomas Edison and the invention of the light bulb or about the Civil War or World Wars 1 and 2. He painted a great picture of what was going on at the time. He also used films which made history class come alive for me. That's because, as I would learn later in life, I am an auditory learner.

We had quizzes every few days and tests every few weeks. He also graded our notebooks. This is where trouble started for me. I didn't know the first thing about how to take notes, so I just did what I thought note-taking was. I wrote down verbatim what the history books said. He said not to do that because it was plagiarism, but I didn't know what plagiarism was. I think he thought I was just being defiant and/or disobedient. When he graded my notebook again, he noticed that I was doing the same thing as before, so he got angrier!

I was blessed in some ways to have Coach M. as my history teacher the next year, but that blessing certainly did not come right away. He began grading my notebook again and I was still doing the same thing. Plagiarism! I still didn't know what it was and I was afraid to ask. This time, he was really angry and said he wanted to see me in the hall. He said what I was doing was against the law and that I could get in a lot of trouble!

By the time he finished yelling at me, I was crying really hard. I said, "Coach, may I speak freely?" He said yes. "I just moved here last year. Prior to that I was in a special education school where we never had to take notes, so nobody ever taught me how! Please help me. I'm not trying to make you mad!"

When I saw the look of surprise on his face, I knew he understood. I wasn't doing well at taking notes or tests in my other classes either. (My grades weren't very good that year.) The difference was other teachers weren't grading my notebook for part of my overall grade.

Lessons Learned from the Bottom of the Stairs

One of my friends and basketball team associates, Mike T., told me what valedictorians and salutatorians were. I asked him if students who compete at that level have to study as hard as, say, someone whose ability to learn does not come as easy. He said that studying comes a little bit easier to them, but they are also more dedicated to what they are doing. They have experienced success…and the desire to succeed builds upon a person's increasing desire to learn more. It also builds upon past successes.

Then I said, "Hey, that gives me an idea! If studying does not come as hard to them as it might come for me, since I have a mild learning disability, maybe some of them would have time to help me learn— how to take notes, study, and do research!" Then Mike said that they might be able to help and it's certainly worth a try.

When I shared this story with Coach M., he agreed, so after I talked to the teachers, they were willing to do anything they could to help me. One of my favorite teachers was Sally D. She was the head of the debate team and worked with students interested in acting and theater production…and she was my public speaking teacher.

(I had a public speaking teacher at Tara the previous year too, but it didn't take me long to discover that she was giving me A's on speeches because she felt sorry for me. I was sure of this because the other students were doing research on the topics they wrote about. I told my teacher I didn't understand how I got an A.)

But I liked Sally D. from the very beginning. I told her about my previous teacher and she said, "Randy, I don't give A's because no one is perfect. And I don't give F's unless you refuse to try, because no one is a failure." Then I smiled at her and said, "Okay, then I'm just going to make the highest B I can make in your class!" And she smiled back.

When she saw me struggling with her tests, she was the first of my teachers to ask me to stay after class or make arrangements to take my tests orally. Later a few other teachers asked me to do the same thing. That's when I discovered I was a verbal processor and an auditory learner, but I did not completely wake up to the idea of it myself until many years later after I became a Christian and attended Open Door Fellowship! By then I was 40 years old. I tried to read books because that was what my mom encouraged me to do. But I didn't know how to tell anyone that my eyes were watering like crazy and I might read the same line over and over thinking all I had to do was try harder. I didn't understand the torture I was putting myself through until I woke up to the fact that I loved listening to audio books and lectures.

By the way, when I graduated, I earned a B+ + + in Mrs. D's class. She gave me motivation to learn! She gave me ideas on how to research speeches I was writing. I could tell through the tone of her voice that she was pleased with my effort. Through that, I could tell she loved me as a student and wanted to see me grow as a person!

My teachers gave me the names of various students to help me. Some of them, like Lyn, Emily S., Steve B., Yvette G., and a few others, were already willing to help me because we had developed friendships. I discovered that I gravitated towards people who were smart and loved to learn, but it was not until I grew in my faith and began to find my identity in Christ Jesus, that I believed that I was also very smart. God simply had some hurdles that He wanted me to clear—to learn to rely on Him.

Lesson Learned: It has been said many times that Christ does not call the qualified, He qualifies the called. See 1 Corinthians 1:27-29.

As I started to feel better about my grades and myself, my confidence began to grow. I was sensing that some of the things my friend Mike had shared with me were in fact true. Success was building upon success and confidence was building upon confidence.

I didn't talk to my parents about why students were coming over and hanging out in my room. I was afraid I might get in trouble for not trying hard enough to do the homework myself. Before my dad got sober a few years later, he told me he thought the teachers were giving me grades because they felt sorry for me. (Again, I'm sure that was only true in one case.)

It should be noted, however, that when he got sober after high school, he said he was sorry that he had said that. He told me I was very smart. He went on to tell me he was jealous because he hadn't brought home half the pretty girls as I did when in school! But I was comfortable bringing home women friends to help me get through school. (If I had been thinking about anything else, I would have been scared to death.)

In my senior year (1978), I was 20 years old. I got special education credits converted into elective credits. I began making B's, thanks to the friends who helped me study. I was in a lot of clubs, on the basketball team, and in Key Club. I was having fun! I graduated before any of the other mainstreamed kids did. My English score on the ACT test was on a college sophomore level.

Lesson Learned: And they told me I wasn't smart enough!!! Persistence paid off.

CHAPTER 14
Lessons of Friendship

The friend I loved and enjoyed the most was Lyn. This is how I met her. Near the end of my junior year, students running for offices in student government began making signs to indicate their candidacy. I was one of those candidates! When speech day arrived, I noticed Lyn. She was playing the piano backstage. As she played, I was reminded about how much I missed my mom back home in Denver. Lyn had beautiful golden blonde hair and a smile that was warm and sincere, but she was somewhat shy and quiet. I have always appreciated her kindness to me.

I had a crush on her in high school but never told her how I felt because I was scared. I was afraid that if she knew how I felt she would run away! I memorized her birth date. I put poems that I wrote in her locker. The intensity of how special I thought she was grew privately in my heart, but I want to make this clear! She was very interested in being my friend and I wanted to be her friend also, but a big part of me wanted more.

I told my friends at school who knew her how special I thought she was. I pleaded with them not to tell her because I didn't want to lose her friendship and then lose everything!

The first poem I wrote to her went like this:

"Tell Me Love,
the glassy look on the sidewalk outside, does it rain or do I cry?

Tell Me Love,
the motion your fingers make when you first see me, are they like the wings of a butterfly intended to fly back and remember?
Or are they like the wings of a bird intended to fly away and forget?

Tell Me Love, tell me."

I wrote this poem during the summer of 1977. I had so many feelings and didn't know what to do with them. Sometimes I felt like crying because I felt love for the first time since those days at Handicamp. I also felt like crying because something inside told me my feelings weren't realistic. And I felt like crying because part of me was angry. I thought, "This is the way it always goes for someone on crutches."

(At that time, my identity was in the other person. This was the case with Lyn as well as several other women as the years went by until I grew to learn what it means to find your identity in Christ Jesus.)

When I graduated from high school, Lyn was a big source of encouragement. Our graduation was held at the LSU Assembly Center. The very floor on which I was graduating was named after Pistol Pete Maravich, *The House That Pete Built*. (On a side note, two good friends, Mike and Kent, bought me the book called *Heir to a Dream*, written by Pete Maravich with Darrel Campbell and Frank Schroeder.)

Here's more on the story of Pete Maravich. I once listened to a taped conversation between James Dobson of Focus on the Family and Pete. Pete shared his testimony on the program.

Then he and Dr. Dobson played some basketball. Afterwards, Dr. Dobson turned to take care of some things and two seconds later heard a loud crash. Dr. Dobson turned and saw Pete on the floor with his eyes rolled back in his head. Pete was gone. The autopsy showed that he had had a defective heart valve from birth and "should" have never been able to play basketball…but he did.

Yet my deepest love for Pete Maravich was not about basketball. It was about his love for his father. His father was dying of cancer and Pete led him to the Lord. It reminded me of my love for my own father, who had encouraged my love for basketball. He installed a basketball goal in the driveway for me, long before I played wheelchair ball.

Lesson Learned: Memories are powerful.

Back to my high school graduation. After I got my diploma, I stepped back to take my place in line, but before I could get there, Lyn stopped me. People were applauding so she said, "Randy! Stop! Look at this! This is for you. People love you! We all love you! Take a moment to enjoy this!!!" This was as assertive as I had ever heard her be in the years I had known her. I stopped and looked up and out towards the audience. And all I could do was cry like a baby. So many friends, including her, embraced me as I wept!

As I was getting to know Lyn, I asked her if she was a Christian and she said yes. I thought I saw something different about her! Even though I was not yet a Christian, something struck me about her. I saw it in her eyes.

Lesson Learned: The eyes are the window to the soul. See Matthew 6:22.

In general, I was scared to death to even think about asking a girl to go on a date with me. I was insecure and honestly thought they would say no because there was something ugly about me. This was in my self-talk because I didn't yet know it was wrong. I would learn later that I was lying to myself and hurting myself seriously in the process!!!

I was effectively telling God He was not telling the truth, which is a lie on my part, because it is impossible for God to lie. See Titus 1:2, Hebrews 6:18, Numbers 23:19, John 1:12, Matthew 6:25-34, and Psalm 139 regarding believing and receiving the truth through Jesus Christ.

Looking back, I can see that God was good and was attempting to draw me to Himself in much the same way that a man pursues a relationship with a woman he is interested in. The major difference is that God, the creator of the universe, had you and me in mind before the creation!

Over the past few years, I've shared with Lyn what I could remember about running for student government. She told me that many of the students had been friends in some cases as far back as grade school, so many voted for each other based on friendship. For some reason, I thought I could win if I ran for vice president. After I did not win, I became melancholy and depressed, but what I hadn't focused on in the beginning was that I did very well. I finished third.

When we made our speeches to the different groups each hour, I gave mine with energy, vigor, and conviction. As I look back, I was happy to have had the opportunity to build friendships with so many able-bodied people.

Lesson Learned: The truth is that all of us are disabled in one way or another when it comes to the cross of Christ, because otherwise we would not need the cross. See Isaiah 53:6, Romans 3:23 and 6:23 and John 3:16.

Over time I became popular at school, which became a downfall for me after graduation because I had sought my identity in those who liked me. I've made many friends over the years. I've made friends with anybody who seemed friendly! Sometimes that included people who didn't care about their performance in life very much. If they were going to be nice to me, I wanted to work hard to be nice to them!

CHAPTER 15
Lessons of Brotherhood

After graduation, I moved to Shreveport for a little over a year to learn independent living skills and take GED classes to supplement my high school diploma. I became roommates with Chuck. He was a friendly person but had a problem with drugs--uppers and downers. He could never sit still. Because of my dad's issues with alcohol and now this, I was beginning to grasp more about what addiction was. I did not become entangled with pornography until several years later, but I knew I was addicted to people.

I began hoping for a new roommate. Not long after that, I met Billy Caston, who was across a pool table from me. He had a smile that wouldn't quit. But this time, even more than when I met Lyn, I could tell there was something different about him. His face literally glowed! As I looked into his eyes, there was a peace about him. He was unlike any other disabled person I had ever seen!

I typically did not have anything to do with disabled people unless we had a mutual interest in sports, but I asked him, with no background knowledge about who he was, if we could be roommates. This was very different for me because at the time, I was prideful, self-righteous, and arrogant about who I socialized with. He replied, "It depends on what we have in common." He told me to take some time and think about it and ask him again tomorrow. The next day we were in the exact same place we had been before—in the recreation room, almost as if we were actors in a movie that was put on pause and then resumed 24 hours later.

I asked him again if we could be roommates, and he again replied, it depends on what we have in common. I told him I didn't know what he meant, so he said to come to his room for a minute. I followed him to his room and sat on a bed and looked at him as he sat in his electric wheelchair across from me. He asked me if I had a personal relationship with Jesus Christ. I said my family was a church-going family but no, I couldn't say I had a personal relationship with Jesus Christ. He asked me if I would like to. I said yes, because I was very lonely and could use some help in overcoming the constant feeling of loneliness! Then we prayed…and I accepted Jesus as my Savior.

After we prayed, I again asked him if we could be roommates. This time he said yes. I learned over time that he was not willing to sleep alone in a room if he did not have a Christian roommate.

We read 1 Corinthians 13, the love chapter, about five times a day for six consecutive weeks. Often, we would either take the word "love" out of the passage and replace it with the name Jesus or take the word Jesus out and put the word love back in. It didn't sink in right away, but Billy was very patient. And oh, how he loved to smile!

1 Corinthians 13:
"If I speak in the tongues[a] of men or of angels, but do not have love, I am only a resounding gong or a clanging cymbal. [2] If I have the gift of prophecy and can fathom all mysteries and all knowledge, and if I have a faith that can move mountains, but do not have love, I am nothing. [3] If I give all I possess to the poor and give over my body to hardship that I may boast,[b] but do not have love, I gain nothing.

[4] Love is patient, love is kind. It does not envy, it does not boast, it is not proud. [5] It does not dishonor others, it is not self-seeking, it is not easily angered, it keeps no record of wrongs. [6] Love does not delight in evil but rejoices with the truth. [7] It always protects, always trusts, always hopes, always perseveres.

[8] Love never fails. But where there are prophecies, they will cease; where there are tongues, they will be stilled; where there is knowledge, it will pass away. [9] For we know in part and we prophesy in part, [10] but when completeness comes, what is in part disappears. [11] When I was a child, I talked like a child, I thought like a child, I reasoned like a child. When I became a man, I put the ways of childhood behind me. [12] For now we see only a reflection as in a mirror; then we shall see face to face. Now I know in part; then I shall know fully, even as I am fully known.

[13] And now these three remain: faith, hope and love. But the greatest of these is love."

I have since learned that the word "love" in that text means "agape" (unconditional love). This is the Covenant Love that carries through from the Old Testament into the New Covenant.

When I learned when Billy's birthday was, I was shocked because his birthday was the same as Lyn's! I saw Christ in both of them through the glow in their eyes and the sense of peace they each possessed.

Almost immediately after I accepted Jesus as my Savior, I got a call from my stepmom, whom, by the way, I call Mother. She said I needed to come home that weekend because my dad had been enrolled in a drug and alcohol treatment program. We would be attending a family treatment session to learn more about the process of recovery for all of us as a family.

I spent a significant amount of time participating in that program, which was run by the chemical dependency unit of Baton Rouge General Hospital. We would visit Dad every day. We learned that all of us needed to recover. Going through this helped me learn more about the seriousness of addiction and how it affects others around you. I got to know other people who were in the process of recovery too.

A lot of the families like mine had a long history of chemical abuse issues. This helped me to know that I wasn't weird and my family wasn't weird. Instead, we discovered the depths of chemical addiction and how far back it can travel, as well as how far forward it can continue to travel if the persons involved try to deny it and bury their heads in the sand. We became involved in Al-Anon and Ala-Teen as my father started attending AA meetings. We all began to grow and change. (Later, I became involved in two other similar groups, Daily Christian Fellowship at Open Door and later, Celebrate Recovery, a Christ-centered 12-step group.)

After my first couple of days at the chemical dependency unit, I boarded a bus to head back to Shreveport. I was excited to see Billy again. I wanted to tell him what God was doing to help me, my dad, and my family! While on the bus, I met what appeared to be a much older gentleman. His name was Joe H. He listened to me, then began to tell me about himself and his story. He told me he was a recovering alcoholic and about his journey towards recovery in Alcoholics Anonymous. He told me he had been on the track team at Louisiana State University. We had track in common since I participated in the Special Olympics in the early 1970's in Denver.

He had been on the LSU track team with Billy Cannon and Jim Taylor. These were significant people in the backfield for the LSU Tigers football team when they won the national championship in 1958, the year I was born! The coach of that team was Paul Dietzel. At that time, it was the only national championship team in college football that LSU had.

As he talked about this, I thought about Colorado being a part of the Louisiana Purchase before it became a state in 1876. I was even more glad to be talking with Joe Harris!

As Joe talked, it was very apparent that he was proud of what he had been able to accomplish. He was also very humble as he told me how alcohol had taken everything away from him, but that then he had gotten sober through AA and had gotten to know Jesus Christ as his Lord and Savior. At that point, I was even more interested in Joe! It was as if he was a bridge between my past with my father's journey to sobriety and the new road I had discovered when I met Billy and accepted Jesus Christ as my Savior.

Joe invited me to come and stay at his house for a weekend if I wanted to. I appreciated the opportunity but didn't take it right away because I was scared. I told him that and he was understanding. When we reached the Greyhound station in Shreveport, he offered me a ride to the Independent Living Center where I was rooming with Billy. After that I stayed in touch with him on the phone. He lived in a city near Shreveport called Bossier City.

I told Billy about how I had met Joe on the bus. I said, "God is real! Jesus is real! He is working in my life!"

The next weekend, Billy went home to visit his brother and family, so I took the opportunity to stay at Joe's house. We read the Bible together. He gave me a framed picture of himself along with Billy Cannon Sr. and Jim Taylor, who, by the way, played in the backfield for the Green Bay Packers in the first Super Bowl! Joe had a personal relationship with Jesus. And I was just getting started.

I did some other fun stuff with Joe. We went fishing on a private lake and I caught two 7-pound bass. On another night, he took me to a Bible study led by a man he knew who once played safety for the LSU Tigers on the same 1958 national championship team. His name was John N. Robinson. Joe introduced me to Mr. Robinson and he talked to me more about the significance of Jesus Christ. He encouraged me through a few passages in God's word. I was overwhelmed by the kindness of the Lord and began crying! I felt a great sense of joy in my heart. Mr. Robinson signed his name in his Bible, wrote a word of encouragement in it, and gave it to me. It still sits on my coffee table to this day. I put tabs in it to mark the books of the Bible, but later I memorized the sequence, plus various verses as well.

For a while, I didn't share about my time with Billy and Joe with my family. I was hanging on to these memories as secrets, because I wasn't sure how my family would respond to them.

The following weekend I went to the State Fair with Billy. I was getting more and more comfortable with him, but in some ways our friendship was still new and I was shy about helping him with certain things. While at the fair, we both agreed that we wanted corn dogs, so we bought one each. After I took a bite of mine, I looked at him and he had a big smile on his face. He said, "I need help with my corn dog!" I said okay and then proceeded to take another bite of mine. Still with a smile on his face, he said with laughter in his voice, "If you don't give me a bite of my corn dog I'm going to die. Do you want me to die?" I said no, but I was nervous, scared, and worried about what everybody else would think if I fed him his corn dog. Then I gave him a bite and the light on his face made me smile and we bonded even more. It was the first time I had ever helped another person to cope with their disability! (Billy had muscular dystrophy.)

This may not seem like much on the surface, but he was feeding my soul with the word of the Lord and with memories that I would never forget, and I was feeding him a corn dog. This is a beautiful portrait of what the body of Christ in action is meant to be, even if you are shy and scared of what someone else might think!

Lesson Learned: One of the best ways to break free from the chains that bind us is to press in to Christ by moving through our fear. It is amazing how God uses our peer relationships to accomplish this.

The next weekend, Billy and I went to the first ever Independence Bowl. Louisiana Tech was playing East Carolina in the game. I remembered my friends at Tara telling me about the Tara quarterback, Scooter Spruill, who led the team to become the 1974 State High School football champions. He went on to play Safety at Louisiana Tech University. I told Billy that maybe this quarterback from my high school was still playing for Louisiana Tech due to a possible red-shirting. I loved my high school AND championship sports, so I was hopeful for an opportunity to meet Scooter. But it turned out that the Lord Jesus Christ had more than I ever dreamed of in store!

Billy and I watched the first half of the game together, then the marching bands halftime show, and there was my little sister Lana in her Tara High School Pacesetter uniform marching right in front of my eyes! I didn't expect her to be there and I don't think she expected me to be there, since we had not spoken to each other about this prior to the game. After she marched, I called out to her and we got the opportunity to speak briefly.

(Now before I tell you what happened next, you need to know that growing up, I always loved watching World War II movies such as *The Sands of Iwo Jima*, *Bridge Over the River Kwai*, and *The Longest Day*, with Frank Sinatra, Peter Lawford, and my favorite, John Wayne.)

A few minutes after Lana left, Billy looked to his right and noticed who else but John Wayne passing out carnations to the disabled people at the game that day. Soon John Wayne was standing right in front of Billy and me! He was asking people in the crowd, "Are any of you smoking? If you are, please stop! I am a living example of how dangerous it is!"

When he finally got in front of Billy and me, he asked us the same question. Billy shook his head and we said no. (I was so excited to meet Mr. Wayne! His real-life name was Michael Marion Morrison.)

I said, "Mr. Wayne, may I ask you a personal question?"
He said, "Sure, go ahead. Shoot straight."
So I said, "Mr. Wayne, do you know Jesus Christ as your Savior?"
He replied, "I sure do! And I'm going to see him very soon!"

The game we were at took place near the end of 1978 and he died shortly afterwards, in 1979.

Lesson Learned: Be bold! This was the first attempt I had ever made to be bold while I was so young in my faith.

A few months later, I woke up early one morning to find the lights shining brightly in the room. They were putting Billy on a gurney to take him to the hospital. I asked Billy where he was going and he said, "Randy, I'm not feeling well. I'm going to the hospital, but don't worry, I'll be back! Promise me you will pray, okay?" I agreed and with that they pushed him out of the room and into a waiting ambulance.

I began to pray regularly three times a day. After a week or so I hadn't heard from him, so I called the hospital. They said he was in serious but stable condition. I kept my prayer routine going and called the hospital faithfully each day.

For a week and a half they told me he was in serious but stable condition. After that, the front desk told me he was stable but improved! And they said the same thing every day for another week as I continued to pray. One of the staff people where I was living shouted out to me that I better accept reality because Billy was going to die soon! But I shouted back with conviction, "He is my friend and I promised him I would pray!"

For another week, the front desk at the hospital continued to tell me he was stable but improved.

Then one day when I called, they told me he had just become conscious and had woken up that morning. I asked to talk to him with a sense of longing in my heart.

They said, "Well, usually only family members are allowed to talk to him, but you have been faithful to check on him every day for a long time. We're not supposed to do this, but you may talk to him, but only for a minute! And I mean only for a minute!" I said, "Billy, how are you?" He asked in a severely raspy voice full of expectation, "Did you pray?" I said, "Yes I did! I love you buddy! Yes I did!" He said, "Good, keep praying! I'll be home soon!" I said, "I love you Billy" and he said, "I love you too. Keep praying." And we hung up.

I ran around so many of the floors after that saying, "There's good news! There's good news! God is great! You guys are in for a wonderful surprise!" And about one week after that, Billy came home.

We immediately resumed our Bible reading routine and I helped him with some of his ligament stretch exercises. He always looked up at me with that same radiating smile from the Holy Spirit. We continued to listen to music together and talk about beautiful girls that came to mind and laugh and smile together.

After a month, maybe two, the lights came on in the room again. I was as surprised as the first time. Immediately I turned and asked Billy, "Hey buddy, you doing okay?" He turned on the gurney and looked at me and said, "Randy, I don't feel very well and I don't think I'm going to be back this time, but please don't worry. Please continue to pray! If I don't come back I will meet you in the air!" Then I asked him, "Can I come to your funeral if you do die?" He replied to me because he knew me so well, "No Randy, please don't, because if I die, the body in the casket will only be my flesh and then you won't think of all the times we shared, and you will be sad! But remember when we die our spirit goes on and rests in the presence of the Father."

I was sad, but I knew what he said was true. He didn't want me to become depressed and then dwell only on the past. From our past discussions, he knew I had a tendency to do that very thing. I looked at his picture that I carried in my wallet until somehow it got wet and I couldn't carry it anymore. A few days later he passed away.

Lesson Learned: God steers your life like the rudder of a boat through special relationships if you always remember to let Him have complete control of your life.

After Billy died, I moved back home to Baton Rouge with Dad and Mother. From there, I moved into a halfway house (in Baton Rouge) for people who were in recovery like my father. The opportunity to stay there was set up by my Vocational Rehabilitation counselor. It was also at the advice of my father. I learned some skills but didn't understand what I had in common with the residents there, partly because I was not yet aware of my own addiction issues. I can't say I was emotionally invested in what I learned there since I was not excited in the least about living alone. I went through the motions, however, and completed the program.

Many times my father and I would cross paths and be in the same open Alcoholics Anonymous meetings together. I had built some friendships in Al-Anon and went to some open AA meetings just because I wanted to, but because my father was still in the early period of his recovery, this created occasional tension between us (as well as my step-mom) since we were frequently under the same roof.

Not understanding the lordship of Jesus Christ was difficult for me and it was amplified because Billy was gone. Part of the problem was that, again, my identity was not in Jesus Christ. It was in the security of the quality time that Billy and I had spent together. I wanted things to be different, but God still had more to show me and teach me before that would happen.

CHAPTER 16
Lessons of Guidance

Not long after that, I got my first real steady job at Jobs for the Handicapped. It was a telemarketing job selling long-life light bulbs over the phone. In 1981, I asked for a transfer from the Jobs for the Handicapped site in Baton Rouge to the site in Denver. I moved in with Mom but began having some of the same issues with her that I had had with my dad and stepmom. She started encouraging me to move into my own home. I would sabotage her efforts to teach me to cook because I didn't want to leave. Every time she scheduled a date to teach me to cook, I would take off with my friend from Fletcher Miller School, Terry H. This happened five or six times. I was scared to death to live alone. I felt so isolated. I thought marriage would solve everything. I came to the brink of suicide.

At this point, I got an apartment with Terry at 46th and Kipling (the Camelot Apartments). Neither of us could afford a bed so one of us slept on the box springs and the other slept on the mattress. I talked him into working for Jobs for the Handicapped with me and then we both got an additional job together doing telemarketing and fundraising for Easter Seals.

Neither of us knew the fundamentals of house cleaning and we were both beginning to wear on each other. We worked the same jobs and didn't have much time apart. We agreed to separate in the interest of saving our friendship! Terry moved back home with his parents and I stayed in the apartment until our lease expired. Then I moved back home again briefly before I took up residence in a hotel on West Colfax. I called it the Roach Motel. It was a hard place to keep clean and there was no privacy. You could hear the arguments and intimate moments of your next-door neighbors being expressed through paper thin walls!

I wasn't there long before the owner of the hotel and his wife, who I had come to know, told me I should move because they had gotten fired and would no longer be running the hotel. They helped me find a new residence at 10th and Sheridan. I have two memories there. I learned about a tornado that jumped over my apartment and landed somewhere beyond Colfax. I had a similar experience a few years later while I was living in downtown Englewood. The second memory is about The Way. Here's the back story.

My friend, Terry, and I practiced soccer together at Sloan's Lake. One day, some girls came over to invite us to join them at a nearby picnic and Bible study afterwards. Terry stayed to enjoy the food but after that he wanted to go home. I wanted to stay (because the girls were attractive). Some of the men in the Bible study said they would give me a ride home.

This was anything but a non-denominational Bible study! But it would be a while before I would find that out. The leader of the study talked about a man named Dr. Paul Wierwille who had been given "special revelation from God" about the true meaning of the Bible. He had supposedly been given superior knowledge to that of Jesus Christ. The sect was called "The Way" and was based in Ohio.

I went to subsequent studies, but what held my attention the most was the beautiful women who gave me special attention. I was allowing them to capitalize on the fact that I felt very lonely, but nothing inappropriate took place, sexually. However, I was acting out of desperation and giving in to the desires of the flesh, the way even a Christian who isn't practicing self-control or surrender to the will of God might.

I was only part of the group for two weeks or so. They challenged us to not listen to our parents or any outsiders because Dr. Paul had special revelation from God. They also said the only acceptable translation of the Bible was the King James version. The name "The Way" came from Acts 9, about Saul guarding the coats of those who were stoning Steven. The Pharisees did not view Jesus as God, so they minimized the group of people who became known as Christians and called the movement "The Way." I think it was probably a convenient name for the group I belonged to because they read the book of Acts a lot. In fact, I don't recall them reading much of anything else. The reason the Pharisees referred to the followers of Christ as "The Way" is likely because they heard Jesus refer to Himself as the way, the truth, and the life. John 14:6

Mom kept hearing me talk about The Way so she investigated. Mom called her priest, Jim M., who told me about The Way. They had taught disciples to turn on their parents and kill them. They were very controlling. I didn't have any reason to doubt what I was learning. I see a similarity in the fact that Saul, before he became a servant of Jesus Christ, killed many Christians. However, a Voice interrupted Saul on the road to Damascus and asked him, "Why are you persecuting Me?" Saul was caught up by a bright light into the third heaven and Jesus identified Himself as the one Saul was persecuting. Through this event, Saul became blind, so the Lord sent Ananias to restore Saul's sight. The Holy Spirit had given Ananias the power to do so. You can read the story in the book of Acts.

I was foolishly misled and blindly excited about "The Way" for an unhealthy reason—that I belonged to a group of able-bodied people. However, I was getting alarmed by the group because one morning I left my hotel door unlocked and they took various things that I owned and scattered them all over the house, like forks, knives, pots, and pans. They came over and told me they did it to teach me a lesson to keep my front door locked. Common sense told me that this is not something loving people do to teach someone a better way.

Once I knew that they taught their members to turn against their parents, I felt I had let my mom down, and I loved my mom more than anyone I ever knew. However, Mom had a "maternal instinct bathed in lots of compassion!" She spoke softly and gently to me. She said, "Take your hands down from your eyes, sweetheart!" And as soon as I did, she said, "You are pretty when you cry!" Then I began to cry harder with apologies and love for my mom.

Later she told me that she saw Jesus and Satan in the room, Satan on one side and Jesus on the other. I told Mr. M. I didn't want to go back to the group but there were still some details to work out, murky and dark waters to navigate through.

Mr. M. told me he wanted me to go to a special group of people who could help me with the de-programming process of leaving a cult, and my defenses went up! I told him I was grateful for what I had learned from the Catholic Church but that I didn't want to go back to it right then. To my surprise he told me he wasn't going that direction, but wanted to send me to Bear Valley Baptist Church instead! I was excited and scared at the same time. A Baptist church was somewhere I had wanted to go, but my stepfather argued against me leaving the Catholic Church I was just looking for a place where I would hear "Jesus loves me, this I know."

Mr. M. got down on his knees beside me. "Randy, does your mom love you? (Yes.) Well, she called me about the cult. You can go anywhere where Jesus Christ is at the center, and it will be ok. You won't go to hell. I'm a priest and I'm telling you the truth."

So I went to the anti-cult group and met with the director, Kathy B. Then I went and lived with a lady and her husband who ran a Christian Community Home. The purpose was to make it hard for the people in the cult to find me, yet much to my surprise, they did find out where I was. The leaders of the Home called the police to make sure they didn't come back.

Little did I know that this experience in community living would foreshadow community living through Bear Valley and Open Door Fellowship in my later years.

After that, I went to New Orleans to get away from the cult and also to take micrographics training through Goodwill Industries. This was at the request of my Vocational Rehab counselor, Ann B., to further ensure they would forget about me in due time. I was supposed to get a job in micrographics, but shortly after I learned about the technology, it was already beginning to phase out as a viable industry. I wasn't going to church at this particular time because I mistakenly believed that church was somewhere you went when you were in trouble or struggling in a big way. I did not understand the lordship of Jesus Christ, at least not yet.

(A note about Ann: She and her husband were big fans of the LSU Tigers. Once, they were leaving for an extended vacation, so they gave me their season tickets to the home football games! I called in to the sports radio station each week and said, "I have a free ticket for any lady who would like to take me to the games." It worked for each game!)

Before I left for New Orleans, I spoke with the pastor at Bear Valley Church, Frank Tillapaugh. (I have always been encouraged by those who have been given the gift of teaching through the anointing of the Holy Spirit such as Frank Tillapaugh and later Jeff Giles, Jerry Nelson, and last but not least, my friend, mentor, and pastor, Andy Cannon.)

I gave Frank my phone number and asked him to call me. "It's very important that I talk to you," I said. And he called! That meant so much to me. I told him I needed advice about a church to attend in New Orleans. He immediately gave me information about a church called The House of the Risen Son, not to be confused with The House of the Rising Sun which was a house of prostitution. He didn't want to steer me wrong!

I didn't end up going to that church because I was too lazy at the time, but I will never forget the act of kindness that Frank Tillapaugh showed me. I made a promise and commitment to be faithful to God and to be faithful and grateful to Frank as well as anyone linked to the Tillapaugh family.

During my time in New Orleans, Lyn, who went to college at Ole Miss, once came to New Orleans for a game. I went to the game hoping to see her. I went through the wrong gate (the press gate). They let me watch the game from the press box. I had to stay neutral. "No cheering allowed!!!" said the supervisor. The game was between Ole Miss and Tulane. (I accidentally cheered at the end when Ole Miss won.) I think I saw Lyn but I'm not sure.

I am fortunate today to be able to talk to Lyn. We reconnected 36 years after our graduation. She is happily married today.

After I wrote the poem, "Tell Me" to Lyn, God answered the question of "tell me" with a poetic statement. This is what I said to God.

"Remember me, because it was you who first remembered us. You set a path of redemption before us. When I reflect on what you did upon the cross, I can remember the purpose of the medicine. It was administered on our behalf through your life. It was finished on the cross.

I can't count on a sister or a brother to always be there! I can't count on asking them to always be faithful. Nor can I count on myself to always be faithful to them or to you. I can only confess and repent and through you and your strength, we can all walk through the door of opportunity and start over. No matter how bad it is, you have provided a way out so that we can stand up under it. (1ˢᵗ Corinthians 10:13)

Please continue to teach me how to love you with my life. Please continue to ask me to remember you and what you did on the cross! Because it was you who first remembered us! It was you who first remembered me!

You cause my faith to grow like flowers in the springtime and when I turn to you, you wash my eyes with my own tears and then remind me of the gift of the rain.

I love you, Jesus, I love you! You are the Lord of my Life. You are the Savior of my Soul. As I sit in this wheelchair, you bring me healing and you bring contentment to my soul!"

CHAPTER 17
Lessons of Agony

After I completed the program in New Orleans, I returned to Denver and lived with Mom. One day she said, "Today you're going to move into your own apartment!" So I moved into my own apartment in downtown Englewood (Orchard Place Apartments) in May of 1982. I was still working for Jobs for the Handicapped. I worked there until 1986.

One day, I met Donna on a bus going to a Broncos game. She was going through a ministry called Chrysalis, which helped young women break free of prostitution. We became friends. She visited me a few times. I liked seeing her but was putting too many eggs, metaphorically-speaking, in the Donna relationship basket. After a while she wrote me a letter telling me she couldn't talk to me anymore, but she sent the letter to my mom's house because she couldn't remember my address. After I hadn't heard from her for more than a week, I called her, and she told me she couldn't handle my struggles and her own. We hung up and I was seriously depressed, so I tried to talk to her mom. Her mom came to my apartment and told me about her daughter. She tried to comfort me by sharing some New Age ideas on meditation, which didn't make sense to me. I wasn't going to church but didn't see Jesus Christ at the center of this New Age stuff.

I knew I wouldn't see Donna again, so I went to the brink of suicide. I was going to thrust a kitchen knife through my stomach, but I couldn't do it. I literally tried to dive on top of knives that I was holding in my hand. I attempted three or four times before I got frustrated and threw them across the room. (Also, I wanted to go to heaven and I wasn't sure that if I committed suicide that I would.)

After flinging the knives across the room, I threw myself on the floor, crying! I wanted to die but at the same time I was scared to do so because I knew Jesus Christ was real! I was also mad at God. I was lonely and I didn't know how to stop the loneliness! I cried out to God and said, "Okay. I will go back to Bear Valley, but please help me Lord! Help me find somebody to disciple me and help me learn more about who you are. Please God, help me."

I knew I needed people to disciple me, especially men, because I struggled to trust men due to my wounds from chemical abuse history in my family and my parents' divorce. (This is not intended to put a guilt trip on anyone; just to explain my pain.)

Steve Ramp would be the first of many wonderful brothers in Christ who would disciple me. He later married his then-girlfriend, Sandi. I got involved with Navigators, led by Jeff and Pam Giles, and simultaneously got help from Scott W., Kent Mathews, and Wally H. from the adult Sunday School class at Bear Valley.

I started attending Bear Valley Church on Superbowl Sunday, January 30, 1983. I heard the song "Jesus Loves Me!" I was very unstable emotionally and wanted help. I also wanted to attend the Super Bowl party. I remember thinking, "If I don't go to the party, I might not be here next weekend."

Upon hearing "Jesus Loves Me," I began sobbing because it reminded me of the time I heard it when I was seven years old at Calvary Temple. The words to that song have had a lasting spiritual impact on me. I have learned the importance of practicing spiritual defense, similar to what you learn in competitive sports. Offense sells tickets and puts fannies in the seats, but defense wins championships. You have to keep the other team from scoring in order to win. Learning how to tell yourself the truth in the spiritual world works much the same way. You are no match for Satan, if Jesus Christ is not your Lord and Savior. You must first believe and then receive Him as Lord (John 1:12) to win the battles that the Lord already knows you will face!

When you do lose, and you will from time to time, it is important to praise the Lord. This is just as important as celebrating when you win.

Lesson Learned: I definitely desire to be a champion for the Lord Jesus Christ as I trust in His wisdom and His strength through the Holy Spirit!

Lessons of Agony

The song, "Jesus Loves Me," has demonstrated itself to be true in so many different ways as God's hand has guided me through different ministries. These ministries are highlighted in Frank Tillapaugh's book called, *The Church Unleashed*. God chose to bless many potential leaders through the power of His Holy Spirit during this period at Bear Valley Church.

The ministries that impacted me most were, in no particular order, the adult singles class, Navigators 2:7, the work of Randy Fay and his daughter, Alishaba, and last but certainly not least, the Inner City Health Center (ICHC). Bear Valley also gave birth to Mothers of Preschoolers (MOPS) and Open Door Fellowship.

At Bear Valley that day in 1983, I heard Bob and Jan Williams talk about their vision for the ICHC. Bob was my first doctor and Jan was my first counselor when my life began to turn around because of the light of the Holy Spirit. Jan helped me build my self-esteem and my identity in Christ.

I love the persons of the Holy Trinity, but I did not know how to let God take my pain, how to abide in Him in the midst of it, or how to surrender. I saw my dad do it through AA, but I had to sort out how to do it for myself. I didn't know the source or depth of my pain or my addiction issues. All I knew is that I didn't want to end my life…and that I loved God. I know now that there was more to my pain than addiction, codependency, or loneliness.

Lesson Learned: The long, slow, winding road will take the rest of my life for uncovering, confronting, and dealing with these things. Uncovering them is like peeling the layers from an onion. They must be done slowly. The Lord Jesus has been so loving and patient with me.

One of the other people God brought along to disciple me was Kent Matthews. He became one of my best friends. He was the career singles Sunday School leader at Bear Valley Church. I was struggling with porn. He just tried to get me focused on Christ. He emphasized community—lunch, games, concerts—together.

Lessons Learned from the Bottom of the Stairs

At first, I had a "poor me" attitude. All Kent did was listen. He never complained. I asked him how I could better serve others. Kent would say, "Listen to them." He felt his motives weren't so pure because listening to others kept him from talking about himself, so we both worked on our listening skills (and I'm still working on them).

He and I went through a class on listening skills called "Helping Five" together, taught by Jan Williams. He never judged me. He just waited for me and kept finding ways to make me laugh.

He and another friend, Janet, set up Dinners for 6 and I invited two people. Behind the scenes, he was working to get the guests to get me to talk about myself, but he was asking me to practice focusing on them! I knew then how much he loved me.

He came over to my house to play basketball with me. I ate many Thanksgiving dinners at his house. We went to Nuggets basketball games together as well as Christian concerts and jazz concerts. We also played other sports together including ultimate frisbee. We went to the Urbana Missions Conference together in 1984 which led to three mission trips to Mexico, two of which I went on. These were to Alamos and Novajoa with Food for the Hungry. Team members included Sue, Marilyn, Greg, and Kathy, along with Wally Hollis.

My first job in Mexico was to wipe down tables, but I told them I wanted to do men's work. They sent me out to watch over the water pump. They tried to teach me how to re-start it if it stopped, but I couldn't understand them because I didn't speak Spanish. I was able to learn some Spanish audibly, but struggled with understanding instructions in Spanish. I got stuck when the well stopped because I was prideful and self-reliant, scared to ask for help.

Greg P., a team member, repeatedly taught me how to re-start it. I finally was able to do it. Later, a kind Mexican man, Emiliano, and Greg gave me the opportunity to work on the roof, scraping paint off glass squares called sky lamps. My teammates pushed me up to the rooftop. Again, I didn't understand the task, which was scraping paint off with the back edge of a hammer. Instead, I shattered six of the sky lamps because I thought they wanted to put in new ones. I felt terrible, heaping condemnation on myself. I had not yet learned many of the things that I now know, like 1 Corinthians 1:25-31. God uses the foolish things of the world to shame the wise and the weak things of the world to shame the strong.

That night at church, Emiliano talked over an hour about me, but I couldn't understand his Spanish. He was touched by the Holy Spirit that I would come from America with my disability to serve God. In Mexico, disabled people beg on the corners since there's no Social Security. People who made fun of disabled beggars were blackballed in that community, but Emiliano noted that I had gone far beyond anything expected of a disabled person. He didn't want me to think less of myself because I couldn't meet my own expectations.

Kent also introduced me to TRYAD in 1984. (More about TRYAD later.)

Another inspirational person in my life was Vernon Grounds, who was the president of Denver Seminary and Kent's mentor. Dr. Grounds was an extremely humble man who had time for everyone. I love two things he often said. The first was a quote from a chorus written by John Burton, Sr. "Holy Bible, book divine, precious treasure thou art mine. Mine to tell me whence I came. Mine to tell me what I am."

The other was simply the word "ditto!" I once told him I loved him. He looked at me with enthusiasm and warmth and simply replied "ditto." I thought that was an incredible way to say I love you to someone. I have learned to identify with the face of Christ in my growth and healing through Kent, Dr. Grounds, and Andy Cannon. This is what a friend of mine at Open Door Fellowship, Jarrod Irwin, has been teaching me.

Eventually Kent went to work with Henri Nouwen (L'ark Communities) in France. He went to a retreat there and was riding his bike home when he was hit and killed.

Here I go crying again! I miss him. He was one of the first men in my life (along with Steve, Wally, and Jeff Giles) that I ever deeply trusted. I also miss his mom and dad and sister Cheryl.

Lesson Learned: Like Andy Cannon says, we are only as sick as the secrets we keep. I must feel in order to heal.

CHAPTER 18
Lessons of Balance

Early in my walk with Jesus Christ, I was in a Bible Study with Steve Ramp. I remember commenting to my teachers about how important grace was, yet I told God I did not want grace! I was arrogant and prideful. I felt I could follow Jesus if I tried hard enough. A friend in the Bible Study named Elaine gave me a book called *Where Eagles Soar* by Jamie Buckingham. It's about relying on the Holy Spirit, not on our own efforts.

Part of the truth was, I was hurting deeply and didn't know it. The other part was that I didn't have the slightest idea how important grace was in the concept of salvation. My prayer life was weak at best. I could identify with the Apostle Paul in Romans 7. "I do the things I don't want to do. And I don't do the things I want to do without God working through me in accordance with His will in the first place."

I worked through most of a book by Gene Getz called *The Measure of a Man* with Steve. He encouraged me to take one step at a time and complete what I started. I loved him a lot! He taught me what a pun is. He did a great impression of John Wayne. He reminded me of the Star Trek series because he would say, "Beam me up, Scotty." I watched him play a lot of flag football and softball. He married Sandi. (I hope you are both doing well. May the peace of Jesus Christ be with you both!)

After working with Steve, Jeff Giles introduced me to the Navigators 2:7 series. The Navigators is a Christian discipleship program. (Jeff later became the head pastor at Hoffman Heights Baptist Church.) I talked to him a lot about my addiction to pornography, but I was spinning my wheels, like a car in a snowstorm. He kept asking me if I thought it was worth it, but I didn't understand how that question would help me stop. I thought something I started but didn't like should be easy to stop.

In Navigators, we spent a lot of time memorizing verses. During this time, a friend named Ed teased me about a tiny naked lady on my

Hawaiian shirt, which I told him wasn't there! But I went to the men's room and looked closely and sure enough, there she was hidden within the flowers of my shirt!

Lesson Learned: It's really important to listen to your elders!

Jeff told me I had to do my Navigators homework, so I started working on back lessons. However, I didn't do so well. He came over to kick me out of the group, but instead said, "Look at you! You just need someone to push you." I was still struggling with how to learn, so Jeff told me he would take me to the seminary library so I could study, then we would go to his house for dinner every Monday. I started memorizing verses. I started learning!

(Side note: One night I was at Jeff's home and he started wrestling with his little son. I pulled Jeff off his little son, Jason, so Jeff turned to me and started wrestling with ME. I started crying because it was one of the first times I felt accepted in a male bonding sort of way.)

I also got to know Wally and Scott during this time. They were kind to me and gave me rides to church. Wally worked for KWBI radio (and later went to the mission field with TransWorld Radio). He taught me a lot about rock-and-roll singers who gave their lives to Christ, like how Jeff Pollard from Louisiana's Leroux led Kerry Livgren from the band Kansas to Christ. He told me about the band Poco and about Richie Furay, founder of the rock group Buffalo Springfield. (I was never able to play the album by Richie that Wally gave me because my record player broke.)

However, years later while at Open Door Fellowship, I went to an event at the Pepsi Center in Denver and wouldn't you know it, Richie was leading worship! The music he played that day resonated with my spirit so much that I started crying. I told my friend, Linda Collins, about him. She already knew who he was, and she and her daughter took me to a record store to find some of his music. We also went to some of his live concerts in Boulder. I read his biography, *Picking Up the Pieces*. Linda threw a beautiful 50th birthday party for me. She told Richie about my birthday and he sent me a birthday email! Linda helped me to grow and understand suffering from a Biblical perspective. She later passed away from a long battle with cancer, but found the strength to celebrate my birthday one more time before she died.

(Linda, I can't wait to see you again in heaven. We can dance together with brand new feet and contemplate the book, *You Gotta Keep Dancin'* by Tim Hansel. I love you Linda!)

My sister, Brenda, married Ted Kleinhans in 1982. Ted was like the big brother I always wanted because of our mutual love of sports. In 1984, I asked him if it would be possible to see a World Series baseball game together. He had Detroit Tigers season tickets, so he and my sister entered a lottery and won an extra ticket. My first major league baseball game was a World Series game! I must have had a silver spoon in my mouth because the Tigers won the World Series that year. I would later see the Colorado Rockies get swept by the Boston Red Sox 4 games to 0 in the 2007 World Series, but at least I got to see my very own team participate on the big stage.

I shared Christ with Ted, but he had a hard time believing in God's love because a childhood friend of his had died in a house fire. Ted couldn't understand why God didn't save him. I just kept being his friend without coming on too strong about Christ.

Later, in the spring of 1986, Ted was diagnosed with multiple sclerosis. (Ted and Brenda were divorced in 1994 but remained friends.) I called him after his diagnosis. He asked me how I had coped with my disability. I asked if he was ready for the answer. He said yes. I told him it was because of my relationship with Jesus Christ. I told him God cared about his soul. I knew he would learn a lot through what he would go through.

(That was the last time I spoke with Ted. After his death on October 17, 1995, Brenda told me a priest had knelt by his bedside and asked if he wanted to give his life to Christ. Ted said yes. In February of 2018, Brenda and Ted's daughter, Rachel, gave birth to a son. He's named after his grandfather. They call him Teddy.)

My sister, Lana, married Brent Brumfield in 1984. 1984 was also the year I was introduced to T.R.Y.A.D., which is the name of our ministry for disabled persons. It is an acronym meaning "to reconcile you able-bodied and disabled" in Christ Jesus. I got to know Pam and Bob Hubbard, Crystal, Carolyn Finnell, Beth M., Robert D., and Kathy B. through TRYAD. Another close TRYAD friend is Dan Foster. I met him at a retreat at Singing River Ranch. Dan co-founded TRYAD with David O'Brien in Oregon.

I played soccer off and on until 1985. At that point, many of the guys who had played soccer together started playing softball. The soccer team had been called the Freebirds, named after the Lynyrd Skynyrd song, so we kept the name and transferred it to the softball team.

I remember one game in particular. I was standing on second base and a player named Bruce Webber hit the ball deep into the outfield. I was running as fast as I could. On crutches. As I came around third base, I tripped over the bag and fell. One crutch flew infield toward the pitcher and the other flew into foul territory near the fence. I was flat on my face and so angry because we needed the score to win. There wasn't time to gather my crutches. All of a sudden, I heard my brother Teddy (who had come to watch) yell, "Crawl Randy! Crawl!" I remember saying, "I can't. They're going to throw me out!" But he kept yelling for me to crawl, so I began digging my hands into the dirt for grip and crawled the fastest army crawl I could ever remember. I think I crawled faster than the crawl stroke I used in the swimming pool! Teddy was yelling "Hurry Randy hurry!" I touched home plate just before the catcher touched my ankle, then heard the umpire yell "Safe!!!" We won the game because of the Lord's help through my brother Teddy.

Lesson Learned: When we pull together as brothers and sisters in Christ, all things are possible. Philippians 1:6. Even while I was crying, I could not give up! I hate to lose, except when losing turns your life around. John Fisher sings about that very concept in an album called *Dark Horse*, that losing is winning if it turns your life around. When you let go of your own self-will and self-reliance, Christ Jesus manifests victory in seemingly impossible circumstances. The blood of Christ and His resurrection can and has turned many lives around. We are not perfect, but we trust in His perfection.

Thank you, Teddy, for reminding me to tell this story. Thank you for your love and encouragement.

There was a time when I wondered as a little boy, "Do ball players really care for disabled people?" The answer is yes. I've had the good fortune of meeting athletes (as well as actors) in the hospital while in a wheelchair or flat on my back in bed.

Is Jesus Lord over my love of sports? In the beginning He wasn't. There was a time when my friends started telling me I was going to sports events too much. They wanted to spend time with me, so I made a decision. I realized that maybe God wanted to use me in ways other than the ministry I have through sports, so I stopped going to as many games.

Lesson Learned: God has used my love of sports to draw me to Himself, but without going to so many games, I've been given many other opportunities to serve God. Balance is the key. It's like juggling. There's always one ball at the top. Within the framework of time, there are different priorities at the top.

CHAPTER 19
Lessons of Sports

From the time I was very little, I can remember my father hitting golf balls from the front lawn into the weedy field on the other side of the block opposite our house. Our family dog, Vic, would chase down every ball. Sometimes Vic didn't know any better, so he would try to catch balls on the fly. If my sisters or I weren't watching Dad hit golf balls, I was watching golf on TV.

As I mentioned before, I did not see my dad again after my early childhood for about nine years. However, I did think of him often as I watched Jack Nicklaus, Lee Trevino, Hale Irwin, and Johnny Miller play golf on television.

When my sisters and I moved to Louisiana, Dad played some golf at Briarwood Country Club, which was near our home. Dad would sometimes take me there and let me sit on the passenger side of a golf cart. He would remind me about caddying opportunities he had had at Cherry Hills Country Club in Denver. I am fairly sure this was during the time that the US Open was played there in 1960.

Once, Dad played golf against Super Bowl 3 champion quarterback, Joe Namath. I was riding in the golf cart as usual, right beside my dad. Dad hit one good shot after another! Joe Namath was with his girlfriend and was getting frustrated because my dad was outplaying him, hole after hole. He said to me with lots of enthusiasm in his voice, "How about your old man?! How about your old man?! How about them apples?"

Back then, Dad was a little scared and unsure about teaching me to play golf, only because there weren't any programs (that we knew of in Louisiana) to help disabled people learn to play golf in the 1970s. Later, however, I heard about one of my friends named Steve Minot from Fletcher Miller School learning to play golf. He had cerebral palsy like me. (More about golf later.)

In 1986, I boarded a plane to talk to Dad about God. That's a lot of money to spend on one conversation! I asked Dad, "Who is your higher power? I want you to be in heaven with me." So he told me his higher power was, indeed, Jesus Christ. Within the last two years, I've asked my dad to please go to church. "I can't get into a car anymore because of my feet and back, but every Sunday I watch Charles Stanley on TV." (That's church!)

My father's mother, Emma Milliken, followed the Lord and encouraged my sisters and me to look toward Him. She never gave up on us even when we rolled down the hill and got grass stains on our clothes! She invited me to visit her apartment after I returned to Denver from Baton Rouge and was living on my own. I was often lonely and was trying to figure out how to cope with living alone.

Just before she died, she taught me a lot about forgiveness. As I said goodbye for the last time, she reminded me about how much I resemble my father in appearance. She told me what a handsome man I was. She prayed with me that God would impact my life for His kingdom and glory. I miss having lunch with her.

She asked me if I would ask my father to forgive her for not being the mother she wanted to be. When I told my father, he shed tears of overwhelming gratitude for his mom and dad.

(I am crying at this moment because I miss my grandma. Pass these words on to her, dear Lord! I love you and miss you, Grandma. The Lord has done a lot to bless me with strength, courage, hope, and perseverance. This is a direct result of your faithful prayers!)

In 1986, I heard about a new wheelchair basketball team called the Denver Rolling Nuggets. I tried out and became the 12th man on the team, meaning I didn't play in many games, but I was on the team for two years! I could hardly catch the basketball, but my teammates instructed me to throw it against the wall and catch it from a close distance. I also went through the grueling task of pushing my manual wheelchair with 4-6 teammates hanging on the back of it. Talk about lactic acid build-up in my arms! But in the long run, the perseverance made me stronger, just like the passage in the Bible that talks about running the race to win the prize.

My roommate on Rolling Nuggets road trips was Jeff D. At the airport, he told me to keep my hands on the top of my wheels as we rode on the electronic walkway. Foolishly, I put my hands on the side rails and my wheelchair tipped backwards. I landed on my back with my feet in the air. The next Monday at practice, my teammates taught me a "listening lesson" by tipping my wheelchair back with my feet in the air and scrimmaging around me for twenty minutes.

Some of my teammates encouraged me to move down to play with the Junior Rolling Nuggets but I told them I wasn't playing for the same reason they were. My reason was that I loved Jesus Christ and wanted to set an example for them to follow. I loved those guys and appreciated the opportunity to be part of the team. They never asked me about my reason again.

I got to meet Michael Jordan during my time in wheelchair basketball.

The Rolling Nuggets often played various high school teams for fundraising and for disability awareness. These opposing teams played in wheelchairs. I had the honor of guarding Mark Randall, a senior at Cherry Creek High School, in a particular game. (Mark went on to play college basketball at the University of Kansas, where they won the national championship. Later, he had a brief stint with the Denver Nuggets.) Unfortunately, when I guarded Mark at that game, I caused his wheelchair to tip over backwards. I thought I had hurt him, so I started crying right there on the court, but he jumped up and gave me a hug and said, "Great play! Keep playing hard!"

During my second year with the team, we finished 15th in the nation and went to the playoffs. We had a home game at Craig Hospital and were ahead by 25 points, so Coach sent me in. I kept passing the ball to better players so I could get an assist (and get my name on the stat sheet), but Coach shouted for me to shoot. I kept passing the ball. This happened several times until he told me he would take me out of the game if I didn't shoot. So just before the buzzer I closed my eyes and took a shot and made it! Coach came running onto the floor and asked, "Did you see? Did you see?" I said, "No, I closed my eyes." He said, "You're impossible!" I was also fouled and went to the free throw line but didn't make that shot.

We went on to play the #1 team in the nation the next week. In fact, they had been #1 for several consecutive years—Casa Colina Rehab Hospital in southern California. We lost that game, but those players commended us on the challenge we gave them. I thank our coach and my teammates Paul, Dick, Jeff, and Kenny. I also thank Barb who helped with fundraising as well as the Denver Broker Restaurant which helped us so many times. I thank Nuggets Coach Doug Moe and some players like Bill Hanzlik, Calvin Nat, Wayne Cooper, Danny Shayes, Mike Evans, Elston Turner, and Dan Issel.

I apologize to one of the best wheelchair athletes I've ever seen, Sherry Ramsey, because I lost my temper and tipped her over. Please forgive me!

Lesson Learned: Jesus wants us to boast in our weaknesses. I was certainly weak in that moment. 2 Corinthians 12:9 – "My power is perfected in weakness. So I will boast all the more gladly in my weakness so that the power of Christ may rest on me."

At my last game with the Rolling Nuggets, my teammates gave me a plaque I still have reads: "Most Inspirational Player-Denver Wheelchair Nuggets 1986-87."

One more point about wheelchair basketball. I got to know Dan Clarke, who has become a good friend. He's a trivia buff. His father, Casey Clarke, was the first Olympic wheelchair basketball coach. Casey Clarke told me that he had only heard of two wheelchair basketball players with cerebral palsy, the second being me. I was really touched to learn this, especially on reflecting upon my teachers at Fletcher Miller who had told me I wouldn't be able to play. I could see the hand of Jesus Christ in this.

During the flight to California to play Casa Colina, I got to know a young man named Fred. I asked him a question. If I were able to get him a ticket to the Super Bowl (at the Rose Bowl in California) if the Broncos made it, would he go? And could I stay with him? As it turned out, the Broncos made it! My sister was able to get the tickets (which I paid for) and Fred and I went with my sister, Brenda, and her husband. Fred also took me to Disneyland!

CHAPTER 20
Lessons of Darkness

The next year, 1988, during the Christmas season, I went through what some people call a Dark Night of the Soul. It was a difficult period in my walk with Jesus Christ. As I have said before, I accepted Jesus Christ as my Savior in 1979, but I did not begin to understand His lordship in my life until a significant amount of time had passed. Part of the learning process unfortunately involved making the same mistake several times before I began to understand and learn from what I was doing to self-medicate. It was a painful process that taught me to trust Christ, no matter what, more deeply! In these pages, you will learn about my addiction history with pornography and how my dreams and fantasies, both good and bad, were woven through the threads of my life. They impacted many of my choices.

My heart was broken over the divorce of my parents! Having said that, I want to make one thing clear. Today I do not blame my mom or dad for the choice they made to go their separate ways! It is not my desire to blame or shame them! I love all of my family—my biological parents, my step-parents, my sisters, and my half-brothers.

I want to communicate about my initial reaction to their divorce that might help you identify with it. A child, or even an adult, interprets and responds to what they are going through, rightly or wrongly. Thank you, Jesus, for your love, grace and forgiveness through your shed blood on the cross!

I had been listening to Chuck Swindoll teach from a series he called "Hope for Those Who Doubt." I shut it off for a day, maybe two. I was angry at God because I thought he loved those who were married more than me. One particular early morning just before Christmas, it was very dark. I was crying because I felt desperately lonely. I said to God, "Why is everybody married or experiencing at least some measure of success in relationships, but not me?" I was crying so hard I thought I was going to get sick to my stomach! I said to God, "I feel like you love married people more than me! Why can't I have a relationship? Why can't I have a marriage? I love you God, but I don't trust you!!! I want to, but I don't know how! It hurts

93

so bad! Help me. Please help me." And I continued sobbing for a while.

Then I sensed the Lord whispering to me: "I knew you didn't trust me; I just wanted to hear you say it!" 1 John 1:9. He then said, "I've got you. I've got you from here," as if He were saying, "Just hold on to Me! And I will hold on to you, even when you are not able to hold on to Me!"

I could sense something different! Certainly I would make mistakes again just like anybody else, but something was different this time. There was a sense of peace in my heart that goes beyond emotion or intellectual reasoning. Hebrews 6:19. But I wouldn't associate this verse with what I was going through until after I met Joni Eareckson Tada in 1989.

When I finally got around to turning the radio program back on, Chuck Swindoll was teaching about Abraham, and about how God was asking him (through a test) to sacrifice his son, Isaac, to the Lord. Genesis 22. I had been failing to understand a very significant thing through this whole process. I was not seeing that God was asking Abraham to offer his son to God as a burnt offering! A burnt offering! That means burn it! And forget it! To surrender what I thought I had a right to, because it belongs to God!

The fact is, it has always belonged to God, but sometimes you and I are just in the process of discovering that these things—relationships, desires, or the longings of our heart—have belonged to Him since before time began.

It is also important to understand how much God hates child sacrifice, but God was still asking and testing Abraham so that He could see Abraham's response. To borrow a phrase that I often hear Joni Eareckson Tada verbalize, "God permits what He hates to accomplish what He loves! "

When we look deeper into this issue, we can see that Abraham's trust went a long way. He understood that God hated child sacrifice, but he also understood that if necessary, God would raise Isaac back to life. He understood that Isaac's life, and then the direction of his life, were in the hands of God, even before he held the knife to Isaac's throat and heard his Lord say, "Stop!" Afterwards, Abraham turned and saw a ram in the thicket and sacrificed it there to the Lord. According to God's word, that place is called "The Lord Will Provide."

However, in the beginning, I did not understand what the Lord was trying to communicate. What I initially comprehended about this story was this: put what you think God is asking you to sacrifice on the altar. If it returns to you, meaning the desire is still there, then I (or anyone else going through the test) would be able to expect that God would meet their desire.

As I look back, my attitude was that God was a celestial gumball machine. If I put in my coin, I would get what I want. But as it turned out, I realized two important things.

1. My motives connected to my desire to be married were screwed up in the first place, in part because I was looking for marriage to make my pain go away, i.e., another attempt to self-medicate.

2. I had questions that I should have asked, but I know now that I didn't ask them because I was not ready to handle the answers.

As a result, God still had other lessons or tests that He would put me through to challenge and change my perspective.

You will see God speak to me through my pain later, through my friendship with Heather Seaver Reed beginning in 1999, as well as through what I am discovering about codependency. You will also see it in my poetry. God the Father, through his son Jesus Christ, is extremely patient with us and longsuffering in His love for us!

Lesson Learned: His desire for us is not that we should suffer for eternity but have eternal life!
2 Peter 3:9 and 2 Corinthians 1:3-11

So, the understanding I gained about the story of Abraham and Isaac continued through that evening and a significant amount of time forward.

Later that same night, I went to the Safeway grocery store near where I lived, halfway between Craig Hospital to the east and Cinderella City shopping center to the west (in December of 1988). After making a purchase at the store, I headed for home with the grocery bag hanging from my crutch handle. As I was making my way across the parking lot, I lost my balance slightly and fell to my knees. My first thought was to turn my body around and walk on my knees towards the wall of the store.

But just then, with the lesson called "Hope for Those Who Doubt" still on my mind, another idea crossed my mind! I am sure it was from the Lord. I thought, "Hey, this is an opportunity to trust God with my disability." I had trusted God in small ways, but this was a "Mount Moriah" issue, one that is very closely tied to the insecurity I felt about not being married (in association with my codependency issues).

I asked God if He would show me a sign that He would take care of me and my disability. I was throwing a fleece before the Lord just as Gideon had thrown a fleece before the Lord. See Joshua chapter 6. I looked up towards the sky and thought about the stars that I could see, remembering at the same time what God had said to Abraham, which was that He would make a great nation out of Abraham, a nation that would outnumber the stars.

I reminded myself that I was part of that promise that God made to Abraham, because by faith, I was a Gentile among many others who were grafted in to the Vine. See John chapter 15. I understood then that it is very important not to take throwing a fleece before the Lord lightly!

Lesson Learned: How God chose to answer my prayer was up to Him. He is God and we are not!

I waited a few minutes and then a car pulled up a few feet in front of me. A lady leaned her head out the window and asked if I needed help. I said yes, so she got out of the car and came up behind me. She said, "Okay, I'm a physical therapist. I'm going to put my arms around you and bend my back and bend my knees. At the count of three you will be up on your feet." And that's just what happened. She then went into the store to shop and I started walking the short distance towards my apartment. But I was walking slowly, contemplating what had just happened a few minutes before. Tears were slowly beginning to fall from my eyes. As slow as my footsteps.

Then, just before I got to my apartment, the lady who had just helped me drove up and asked, "Do you need a ride home?" I said, "I don't need help, but I want a ride, because I want to share with you how you have just helped me." I shared some of the issues I had been struggling with and told her about the pain I had felt earlier that morning.

I didn't know whether or not she was a Christian. I intentionally didn't share the gospel with her, because there was still one question on my heart that only the Lord knew the answer to. I just said, "God bless you!" I was intentionally trying to be generic, to see how she would respond. And she said, "May the peace of Jesus Christ be with you!"

It was clear to me at this point that my Savior was behind everything that happened that day. I was stunned and yet filled with joy! I prayed to God, thanked Him, and asked Him to strengthen my spirit and help me to grow stronger in my faith. I continued to sob, overwhelmed yet joyful!

Lesson Learned: This is the day that the Lord has made. We will rejoice and be glad in it. Psalm 118:24.

CHAPTER 21
Lessons of Wilderness

In 1989, I started attending Southern Gables Evangelical Free Church. I met some wonderful brothers and sisters in Christ there, like Landy and Kathy Williams, Dean Wertz, Chaz Bauer, Rich Blum, Randy Allen, Jeff Wiechman, Chris M., Karen Meyer (now Crowfoot), Nancy Nielsen, Barb Light, Cathy Cubbin, and Karen Plemons, and others. The head pastor was Jerry Nelson, who challenged my thinking in terms of serving…and regarding the benefit of suffering for Christ's glory and honor.

Jeff Wiechman was one of a few men that I learned to trust in the early years of my walk with Jesus. Of course, Billy Caston was the first, in 1979, but my walk with Jesus did not really begin to take off until 1983. My lack of trust in men says a lot about my insecure feelings as the oldest of five siblings.

During my time at Southern Gables, there were several significant outdoor wilderness experiences, led by Jeff Wiechman, that I took part in. We went on two horseback riding trips at Red Feather Lakes above timberline near Fort Collins, Colorado. There were three men on this trip and four women. Two of the men, myself included, were/are disabled. One of the women, Karen, is physically disabled and another woman who was fun to talk to and learn about was Barb. She had a different disability that I will keep anonymous, but she had great leadership skills.

If you've ever seen the movie *Man from Snowy River* and its sequel, you might remember scenes of the sharp, steep descent down the mountainside in both movies. This was what it was like for me! During the first part of the horseback ride, my legs were tight. We made adjustments that enabled me to stand up in the stirrups during the trail portion of the rides, but I had to keep my head back over the buttocks of the horse to descend. For some reason, standing up in the stirrups helped me stretch out and relieve the tightness, yet to relax at the same time. But I forgot about this on the second trip. I was frustrated and angry at myself because I forgot all about the comfort and relief I got from standing in the stirrups. During the second trip, I experienced the same pain, but couldn't remember what to do to relieve it. And that was not something that was common for me to do. Whenever I was in pain in the past and found a way to relieve it, it was important enough to remember! I have been through a significant amount of pain.

Lesson Learned: It's helpful to remember that God doesn't forget! He is perfect and I am human. Because I am human, I will not be perfect until I reach eternity and heaven.

Each time I got off the horse, I was eager to give him carrots for saving my life in some respects because I was so filled with fear at the beginning of the descent. He was protecting me because he was free to protect himself and do what horses do, which is to respond to the rider sitting on his back. This experience went far in me, because it was the beginning phase of experiencing a deeper level of trust in the Lord as well as a deeper level of confidence in myself from the Lord. Finally, it led to a deeper level of trust in my peers, my brothers in Christ. Prior to this, trusting my brothers in Christ (other than Kent Mathews, Jeff Giles, and Billy) was only achieved on a superficial level. The relationship I have with Jeff Wiechman has had a lasting impact on my life.

Here are some words from the song "Fear Is a Liar" by Zach Williams. Even though I heard this song much later in life, the words match the feelings I had about fear on the horseback riding trips. Fear can stand for "false evidence appearing real." This is attributed to Satan. But I came up with another acronym about our fear in the Lord, meaning awe of the Lord: "faith evidence appearing real."

Another of our group activities was riding behind a dog sled in Frisco, Colorado. Jeff taught me that for every dog that is connected to a dog sled, you can travel close to one mile per hour, although there are variables such as wind speed, temperature, and overall conditions related to the dogs and the environment. I got to stand in front of Jeff, where I could feel his support behind me and still have a chance to maintain control of the sled and the dogs in front of me, which was exhilarating.

I have always had a deep love for dogs that goes all the way back to our German Shepherd, Vic, when we lived in the Pink House. Vic, on more than one occasion, was my pillow when I was exhausted from using my arms to climb the ladder of the slide on our swing set, then sliding down and crawling through the gravel all the way back around to the other end, then pulling my way up the ladder with my arms again and again so that I could go down the slide again and again. When I was too exhausted to do it one more time, I fell asleep with my head on his stomach. He was there if we wanted to play and he was there to lick our tears away if we were sad.

This is just another way, when I look back on it, that our father demonstrated through his actions that he loved us. He got Vic to protect us and that's what Vic did! I can't tell you how much forgiveness has done to bring reconciliation between me and my father, not to mention a deep and satisfying affectionate love for him! I love you, Dad. This part is dedicated to you.

When Mom took us to the grocery store, Vic would follow her car and she would feel compelled to make sure he made it home safely. She would pack the groceries in the back seat along with my sisters and the dog and all. I would see everything through the rearview mirror and smile. Vic was family. Everybody felt that way. When I got older, I began to grow very interested in Huskies because they looked so much like wolves. How wolves function as a family is fascinating to me.

It has been a long but beautiful journey to learn how to trust men instead of falling into the trap of overvaluing women, which began with my mom because of the father wound that developed in me from childhood. (The same thing happened to my father as well.) I am grateful to the Lord for how He has used so many different men in my life to bring me to a deeper and healthier trust in my brothers in Christ! I can't mention all of you here because someone who doesn't deserve it would be left out, but those of you who know me, those of you who have challenged me, those of you who have listened to my tears and still helped me to laugh, you know who you are! May the peace of the Lord Jesus Christ be with each and every one of you!

Still another experience I had with Jeff Wiechman was going to hear Tim Hansel speak. Tim was a tenderhearted man with a deep love for Jesus Christ. He was climbing and fell seven stories through a crevasse. He had to climb out on his own or die. In climbing out, he did irreparable damage to his back. He had to learn to manage chronic pain for the rest of his life. He became a motivational speaker who ministered to people like me because I had a tendency to feel sorry for myself because I wasn't married.

As Tim told his story, if he cried, I cried. If he laughed, I laughed! Jeff was trying to get me to understand that sharing your feelings was good therapy, yet the best therapy was learning to put your disappointments behind you, and then move forward with God! I learned about how Tim dealt with pain—emotional pain, psychological pain, not to mention physical pain, while being thoroughly honest about it. I appreciated it the most as I read his book, *You Gotta Keep Dancin'*. For me that is saying something, because I have not read a lot of books.

Lesson Learned: Suffering is a gift. You give it to God. My job is to surrender, even though God's answers may not be what I would have thought.

Also during my time at Southern Gables, a friend named Chris started a discipleship group. Some of my friends were invited, but I was not. When I asked Chris why I wasn't invited, he told me he was concerned that I was a name dropper, meaning someone who enjoyed finding security in who they met such as baseball players or famous people. I prayed and realized there was a measure of truth to what he was saying. However, in the past, a number of athletes had shared the gospel with me, and God had opened doors for me to share the gospel with athletes. Has pride been an element in my communication with athletes? Yes! At times communicating the gospel was an attempt to prove that I was smart and important. I'm not proud of that. Sometimes I have come up short in attempting to reflect the glory of God. Rationalizing behavior is an example of being out of step with the Holy Spirit.

When we start a group, all members of the church body should be included (except where gender might be a dividing line). That being said, Chris was a terrific leader, especially in one-to-one situations.

Lesson Learned: Peter and the disciples sometimes were also out of step. But when we are aware of our weaknesses, we must not be afraid to go to Jesus and in doing so, let our weaknesses be our strength.

CHAPTER 22
Lessons of Promises

During this time, Jesus Christ encouraged me to address another problem that can become big if we do not treat one another as equals, which can bring harm to the church body without realizing it. I thank a dear friend for listening to me about something that was unintentional on his part. Because of the way he handled it, I grew to become more of a man of courage and conviction. I grew in two ways. I was less insecure about speaking to others regarding matters of integrity. And I was strengthened to listen to others more frequently.

Lesson Learned: One of my frequent shortcomings is to give in to the urge to speak, even interrupting someone who has the floor. It is a form of fear. It's also a form of self-righteousness that is related to pride. I have one mouth but two ears! I can use your prayers as I continue to learn to use them proportionately. The fact that this friend listened to me has been a source of inspiration in helping me value listening to others. He did not become defensive.

For the better part of a year, when I wanted to encourage this friend and thank him for his input into my life, I would get his attention and he would reply, "What do you need?" I didn't need anything. I began to feel like an imposition. I was taught in counseling to check out my feelings and perceptions with others, so once more I went up to him and he asked, "What do you need?" This time, I did need something. I needed an answer. I needed to know why he assumed that I always needed something.

I try to be careful about always telling people what I need. I would like to give to others more than they give to me. It is easier said than done because of my disability, but I want to be remembered more for what I give than for what I receive.

He immediately said he was sorry. He didn't realize he was coming across that way and he said he would be more careful in addressing me and other disabled people as well. I looked into his eyes and saw sincere sorrow and repentance.

I really like him. I like to thank people that I am learning from. I told him it wasn't my intention for him to feel hurt, but he said, "No, Randy, thank you for your courage and for sharing your insight and perspective." Then we shook hands, embraced, and prayed together.

Lesson Learned: Let all of us, brothers and sisters alike, look for opportunities to seek reconciliation.

In the late 80's, a friend invited me to go with him to a coffee house started by Open Door Fellowship. It was called "Jesus on Main Street." I had the opportunity to read some of my poetry there and I listened to others' poetry. It was a good time, but I was filled with pride. I wasn't yet aware of my addiction issues and I didn't think I was as bad off as the other people there. This was mostly because I was afraid of "street" people.

Almost immediately after I said that out loud, the Lord spoke back to me in a still small voice through my conscience. He said, "Rand," (which is how many of my close friends and siblings refer to me, ironically when they are about to exhort or encourage me in a loving way), "You don't know what you're missing by being here!!!" So when I was struggling with suicidal thoughts (as I was periodically from 1983 until 1993), the memory of how and what the Lord spoke to me then came back to me.

At the same time, I was pondering conversations I had had with Kent Matthews about community living, especially through recreation, mission trips, listening, and caring. The strongest similarity between Bear Valley and Open Door Fellowship was COMMUNITY COMMUNITY COMMUNITY! I experienced some beautiful elements of community at the other churches I attended, but it was central to Bear Valley and Open Door. The motto of Open Door Fellowship is "journeying together, all the way through to becoming like Christ Jesus."

Lesson Learned: I can't tell you I felt warm fuzzies every moment at these churches/fellowships as I worked to overcome fear. People from Open Door didn't pound on my door when I was hesitant or sad or angry at God. They patiently waited for me. And with every positive step I took, they were there to encourage me, time and time again.

I frequently went to Denver First Church of the Nazarene as well as Hoffman Heights Baptist Church during my time at Southern Gables. I met Sonny W. at Denver First Church. He ran the transportation ministry for disabled people there. Sonny set me up with a "date" with Joni Eareckson Tada, which was really a get-together of brothers and sisters in Christ.

Sonny and I shared a love for the Colorado Buffaloes football team. (At one point, I tried to follow the Colorado State Rams, but I grew tired of seeing them lose. I hate losing!) Anyway, I was able to get season tickets to the Buffs games sitting next to Sonny for one year. In 1989, the starting quarterback died of cancer. Head coach Bill McCartney led him to Christ before he died. Coach McCartney said, "I am not a football coach who is a Christian; I am a Christian who is a football coach." I wept because I too wanted to be a Christian who was an athlete, not an athlete who was a Christian! I hope that is what you see in my story.

I was excited when I heard McCartney was going to interview for the position at the University of Colorado. He was one of the best defensive coordinators in college football. I did not see my first game at Folsom Field in Boulder until the day Bill McCartney beat the Nebraska Cornhuskers, which turned the future around for the Colorado Buffs. I had sensed something good might happen, so I took a bus to Boulder and bought the only ticket I could find, which was a single seat in the Nebraska cheering section. There I sat in my black and gold in a sea of red shirts. The Cornhuskers kept over-pursuing to one side, so I turned to the fan next to me and said that if the Nebraska players didn't stop doing that, the Buffaloes would run a reverse. Sure enough, that's what happened. Jeff Campbell went around to the left on the next play, catching the Cornhuskers off balance, taking the lead, and eventually beating Nebraska 20-10.

Lessons Learned from the Bottom of the Stairs

The Buffs played Notre Dame in the 1989-90 Orange Bowl and lost. Then they played Notre Dame a second time in the Orange Bowl, 1990-91, and won!

In 1990, five of us, most of whom were disabled, went to the Orange Bowl game in Miami to see the Buffs play. Two events took place before the game even started. One was that my four buddies told me there was no room for me to sleep in the hotel, but would I take $25 to sleep in the bathtub. I said no, but when the amount climbed to $225, I said yes. The stipulations were that I had to sleep with no clothes on and if I was caught with my eyes open I would lose the bet. I won the bet which covered the cost of my ticket, hotel expense, and dinner at the hotel!

The second event had to do with standing in line to buy souvenirs. As we waited, someone called to us saying we were invited to the locker room by Coach McCartney. We knew this was the chance of a lifetime so within minutes we were in the locker room. Before we left for the trip, I had told my cousin, Celeste, that we were going to the game and she told me a neighbor of hers was on the team. I got confused and thought she had said a third cousin of mine was on the team. His name was Bill Coleman and he wore #77, and when I saw him in the locker room I called out to him that we were third cousins. He stepped over and shook my hand and gave me a hug.

The funny part is that two weeks ago, as I was clarifying this story with my cousin, she said that Bill Coleman was her neighbor, not a third cousin. I had mistakenly believed this for 28 years! The egg is on my face! Sorry, Celeste and Bill!

Lesson Learned: The common thread in team sports is to succeed as a team through communication and working together. That way, even if you lose, you can apply the lessons you learned at the next opportunity to win. The next most important objective is how to win or lose with grace, humility, and integrity.

I had struggled with pride and anger a lot, even after I became a Christian, but God develops your character as you go along. That's one thing I loved about Bill McCartney. He took ownership of his

108

mistakes. You must believe your sins are paid for every time you confess them, no matter how many times confessing a specific sin may be necessary.

Bill McCartney signed on as head coach at the University of Colorado in 1982. When he signed the contract, the athletic director put in a penalty clause, meaning if he were to leave the University of Colorado to take another coaching job, he would have to give money back to the university. Upon signing the subsequent contract, there was no penalty clause.

Later, he was offered the head coaching position at Southern Methodist University and thought it might be a good move for his family. (A lot of people didn't like his outspoken approach to his faith, by the way, so I reasoned that going to a Christian school might mean he wouldn't have to deal with the people trying to get him to be quiet.)

So despite the fact that there was no penalty clause, a close friend of McCartney's advised him that since he had a contract, his yes should be yes and his no should be no. Matthew 5:37. Out of integrity, he decided to stay at the University of Colorado. I was stirred and moved by this! Why? Because I realized that I, too, was breaking a contract. I was riding the RTD bus but trying to do so without paying the fare. I felt conviction by the Holy Spirit, confessed my sin to God, and began paying my fare on a regular basis.

Later, as I was volunteering at a small Christian school in Bailey, Colorado, I learned that Bill McCartney was speaking there. It was refreshing to hear him tell his story.

Lesson Learned: It's not necessarily about the mistakes we make or almost make, the question is…are we willing to do the right thing? 1 John 1:9

A big blessing I've had was to be involved with Promise Keepers, founded by Bill McCartney. I think the first Promise Keepers event at Folsom Field was in 1992. I wanted to go but had a previous commitment, i.e., to attend a horseback trip at Red Feathers Lake.

Promise Keepers was important to me because I wanted to learn more about loving men for the glory of Jesus Christ!

I also wanted to know more about how to cross racial and denominational lines, but I knew that if I was going to be a promise keeper, I had to start by keeping my word to friends who were investing in people with disabilities and overcoming barriers of fear. So I did that horseback trip and loved it.

But before the trip, I had a desire to encourage Bill McCartney. I called Mr. McCartney's secretary and asked to speak with him. This was just before the Promise Keepers weekend. She said he could call me Monday, but I said, "Ma'am, with all due respect, I want to pray with him about the event and by Monday it will be over." Five minutes later, I got a call and it was Bill McCartney. We spoke for a while and I asked him, "What is one area of your life when you are coaching football, or living life outside of football, that you need prayer for?" He answered, then asked me how he could pray for me and I told him I needed prayer for my addiction to pornography and for financial integrity and honesty. Then we prayed together. I was blessed by God with the opportunity to participate in the next three Promise Keepers events.

Lesson Learned: God desires to bless us when we're willing to face the truth about who we are.

CHAPTER 23
Lessons of Joy

Around 1991 or '92, I heard about "Golf for Fun." I was listening to a sports talk show on the radio and heard about this program which brought disabled and able-bodied people together to socialize and have fun, while at the same time, learn to play golf. Our coach at Golf for Fun was a nice lady named Marsha Bailey. She is a member of the Colorado Golf Hall of Fame and was a teaching pro at Raccoon Creek Golf Course in Littleton, Colorado where we practiced.

Golf for Fun started when a young lady named Nan Wolbert, who had just had a stroke, was trying to do something therapeutic. (She also wanted to get out of the house!) She asked Marsha, "What if we could get some other disabled people involved in this too?" Marsha replied, "That's a great idea!"

When I first became involved with Golf for Fun, I was discouraged because I couldn't hit the ball no matter how hard I tried. I had never given up on any sport other than snow skiing. Determined not to give up, I called a dear friend, Sam Andrews, who was head of the Recreation Department at Craig Rehabilitation Hospital at the time. He scheduled time to come out to see if he could help me. And wouldn't you know it, that very same day, other coaches I had not yet met came and introduced themselves to me. It was as if God was opening a door to usher me into the game of golf. I would no longer be contemplating the game in my head from my couch or seated in a golf cart next to my dad. Now I could contemplate the game on the course itself because I was playing golf!

Two of my classmates/teammates with Golf for Fun were Nancy O. and Tom H. Nancy was blind and Tom had lost the use of his legs in an accident. Unfortunately, he also lost his marriage because of the accident. Sometimes, when things like that happen, those we think are closest to us surprisingly cut-and-run. I have also cut-and-run when I got confused, discouraged, or frustrated. I'm still learning to overcome it by learning to talk about how I feel. I've also learned to listen to and value the feelings of others when working through this process. To each person who knows about this character flaw in me, thank you for your forgiveness!

But Tom, after dealing with this adversity, raised his children on his own and got into the business of designing a special wheelchair that would raise the occupant to a standing position while still being able to drive the wheelchair! He used this particular wheelchair around the house but also used it, with its unique design, to hit golf balls a long way! And when I say a long way, I mean 200 yards away!

I was still on my crutches when I was learning to play golf. Tom invited me to try out this new wheelchair. When I hit the ball in his wheelchair, I was able to hit it fifty yards further than when I stood on my crutches. When I hit the ball using my crutches, I hit it 125 yards consistently. While using Tom's wheelchair, I could turn my hips slightly because there was a bar I could hang on to with my left hand. This naturally helped my upper body rotate to the left. My right-handed swing would end up touching my left shoulder to finish my follow-through.

Tom got the opportunity to travel and play a round of golf with Arnold Palmer one week while the rest of us were practicing at Raccoon Creek. A short time later, all three local television networks came out to film us as we were learning at Golf for Fun. The Rocky Mountain News, a local morning newspaper at that time, also came and took a picture of me wearing an LSU shirt at practice that day. As a result, I made a new friend!

This is how it happened. I got a phone call from a man I didn't yet know. His name was Tom Morrison. He wanted to know if I was a graduate of Louisiana State University. I said, "No, I'm a fan of LSU, but my stepmom got a medical degree at LSU as did several other family members." Tom then asked me if I would be interested in becoming an honorary member of the Colorado chapter of the LSU Alumni Association. I said yes. I did that for a few years with him.

I asked Tom if he played golf. He said yes, so I asked him if he would consider playing as a member of my team because I was looking for good players. I learned that his scoring handicap was pretty good! He was a 10. He said yes! He and I practiced together quite a bit to get ready for a tournament. During that time, I learned that he had a fraternity brother by the name of Teddy Caston. I was shocked!! I said, "Tom, that is Billy's brother!" I had been telling him about Billy and about the Lord using Billy to help me come to a saving knowledge of Jesus Christ. To this day Tom and I remain very close! I had the opportunity to be in his wedding and to watch his children grow up.

Our golf team played in that tournament at Pole Creek in Winter Park, Colorado. We finished in the top five. Our team included some of my co-workers at Mile High Cable where I was working at the time. I'm thankful to them for sponsoring our team (although Mile High Cable no longer exists).

Often big golf tournaments operate with a shotgun start, some teams opening their round at the first hole while others open at the tenth hole. Our team started that morning at the tenth hole. My teammates gave me the honor of going first. I was wearing my dad's favorite golf shirt. I was just about to tee off with a 6 wood when I came to a complete stop! There was a red fox with a thick furry tail about 30 or 40 feet directly in front of me. The sun was just beginning to rise. It was Labor Day and absolutely beautiful with a cold nip in the air. It all resembled a fine oil painting, but it was a live portrait, one that only God, the Creator of the universe, could paint!

I looked at the beautiful red fox in front of me. I stood there and appreciated him/her. I didn't want to swing at my ball with the fox standing where it was. Soon it slowly walked away. I looked up at the sky, weeping. I couldn't ask for anything more. The Lord Jesus blessed me with a beautiful gift, a live portrait of art!!!

One of the news stations included a picture of me at sunrise on the first hole of that tournament. What a day! And I had a chance to do two things even I thought I would never do. First, I played tournament golf, but most importantly, before the tournament, I had had the chance to play golf beside my dad!

CHAPTER 24
Lessons of Trust

I started attending Open Door Fellowship on a regular basis in 1993. Let me tell you more about Open Door Fellowship. It had its roots in Bear Valley Baptist Church. Open Door Fellowship was started by Andy Cannon and others. Its partner program, the Denver Street School, was started by Tom Tillapaugh. (The Denver Street School is where I would share my struggles with the students in order to help both them and me bring dark things into the light so Satan would flee.) These ministries were housed together to help street people and high school dropouts. Now the Denver Street School is in a different location and not connected directly with Open Door Fellowship or Open Door Ministries.

By the way, Tom Tillapaugh, Frank Tillapaugh, and Linda Cannon (Andy's wife) are all related.

Open Door Ministries is the outreach arm of Open Door Fellowship. It runs programs such as a daycare for children and many of the homes. A few of the other homes are run through the Providence Network in association with Open Door Fellowship. Residents of those homes, as well as some staff members, attend Open Door Fellowship.

In 1993, I was 35 years old. That was the year I began unraveling and overcoming my addiction to pornography through the ministry of Open Door Fellowship. I also grew to understand that because I had been on Social Security Disability since graduating from high school, I had a lot more in common with street people than I thought. I grew to learn how not to paint all those who needed help as street people. After all, I wasn't from the streets, so why should everyone else
who needed help be labeled that way? (Unless, of course, a specific individual identified that way because it was, in fact, the truth.) Amazingly, after a few years, I grew to understand and love so many people who come from so many different backgrounds!

As you know, my pastor, mentor, and friend is Open Door's pastor, Andy Cannon. I love the tenderness, compassion, firmness, and boldness that the Holy Spirit communicates through Andy. He often tells me I'm not the only one being mentored. He reminds me that I am a mentor to him and that I help him understand and empathize with those who are disabled.

During my early years at Open Door Fellowship, I got to know Andy and his wife, Linda, plus their children. I got to know Kevin and Lisa Grenier, Tom and Yvonne Tillapaugh, worship team people like Lorna, Bev, and Crystal, leaders like Mike Ellis, Bruce and Karen Duell, Jim Cessna, missionaries Jon and Meta Nelson (missionaries in Saragosa, Spain), and David and Sonja Elkins. David and I talked football and he urged me to go deeper with Christ Jesus.

I loved the way we worshipped and asked Jesus to come and be with us. The more I attended Open Door Fellowship, the more comfortable I got. We were encouraged to listen closely with compassion in our hearts, to let the Holy Spirit be our guide. Even our leaders shared openly about their needs for prayer.

Lesson Learned: We are all affected by sin. It is important to keep short accounts with God and to confess our shortcomings with someone we trust.

During my early years at Open Door Fellowship, we met for a Sunday night Bible study we called House Church. It was led by Glen and Cindy Westfall and co-led by Tom and Yvonne Tillapaugh. Carolyn Finnell and Beth Morrissey also attended the House Church.

Cindy Westfall also taught Sunday School at Open Door Fellowship. Sometimes, when she was teaching, she picked up on my struggle to focus and would quietly, while teaching, without missing a beat, walk up behind me, place one hand on each side of my head, and whisper into my ear, "Focus." She had a way of knowing our weaknesses and was willing to help.

Her favorite book to teach on was Hebrews. At first, I didn't like trying to follow the book of Hebrews because it didn't flow in linear fashion. When I told her this, she was surprised. I asked why. With gentle and calm confidence she said, "Because Hebrews is written just the way you talk!" She went on to explain that the writer makes a point, illustrates or amplifies it or paints metaphors, then comes back to the point—in a circle.

After that, she had me! I felt encouraged and felt God understood me in a way I had never acknowledged before. I felt free inside! Cindy told me she was going to take a class on Hebrews. She had been recommended by Craig Blomberg, a professor at Denver Seminary, to be able to get into the class. Most, if not all, of the students were men. I was excited and began to pray for her. She has a teaching style that is encouraging to me. And she helped me fall in love with this book.

One day I went to visit the Westfall family. I loved hanging out with Cindy and Glen and their children Aubrey, Chelsea, and Ashley. Cindy has a way of teaching children to multi-task, which is not something I'm very good at. We were watching television and two of the children were also knitting or doing a chore (maybe folding laundry). Cindy taught them to keep their hands busy and mind occupied while they were watching TV. I wish I had learned this concept when I was younger. It might have had an impact on the effects of my cerebral palsy.

I liked to go to their home to hang out or play computer games like Google Peds, which helped me develop my math skills. I liked to watch Ashley take a running leap into her daddy's arms! Watching them made me long to be married and have children of my own, but at the same time I felt scared and inadequate.

One day, I was standing on my crutches near the entrance to their home and Ashley took a flying leap into MY arms, which knocked me down because I couldn't catch her. Cindy disciplined Ashley sternly and ran over to see that I was okay. I was okay…and this may have been one of the most beautiful moments of my life. Ashley saw past my disability. She treated me just like she treated her own dad! Cindy and I soothed Ashley's tears. Cindy just wanted to teach her to be careful, but I saw the love in that act. Ashley didn't care whether or not I would catch her. She just wanted to leap into my arms. I love you, Ashley. And I love your sisters and mom and dad.

Lesson Learned: I can't wait to jump into the arms of God the Father, the arms of the Holy Spirit, and the arms of my Lord and Savior Jesus Christ!

During these same years, my biological brothers and sisters experienced the life of a disabled person through me by playing around with my crutches or wheelchair. One year, I was in the hospital for cellulitis, a blood infection. The hospital released me to go home for our family Thanksgiving meal. My brother Robert started teasing me. He would push me around extremely fast and tilt me back on two wheels. I would say I was going to fall out and he would say, "No you're not. Don't be afraid to trust me!"

Lesson Learned: There are elements of that in our walks with God every day. Sometimes God takes us places we aren't comfortable going and we feel like things are going too fast, but Jesus says, "You're not going to fall. Trust me."

In my mid-30's I began falling in love with audio books. I was also just beginning my spiritual journey at Open Door Fellowship. Until then, trying to read books was an absolute war! I was able to read a few books like the story of Pistol Pete Maravich called *Heir to A Dream* and *An Uncommon Gift,* by James S. Evans. It's a book about a young Christian boy whose father was a pastor. James had a dual learning disability that made learning in a regular classroom setting very difficult. He had dyslexia and hyperkinesia. It's a small book but a very powerful story that impacted me deeply!

A third favorite book, called *Loving the Broken,* was written by Andy Cannon in 2013. This is a book about loving the poor and the broken and learning to love the poor and broken even more! It's a book about discipleship and how Jesus Christ does not just make converts, He disciples them all the way through! The key phrase is all the way through! Ironically, it is a blessing to know that this was the last book I was able to read by turning the pages myself. It is the last book I was able to read in this way "all the way through." I praise God through Jesus Christ and I look forward to having a new body with new hands in heaven with Jesus! Amen. Until then I will continue listening to audio books!

Lesson Learned: God continues to remind us that He is with us…all the way through.

In 1993, I attended an Open Door prayer group every other Tuesday afternoon. Many TRYAD people attended it. In October, it was my turn to be prayed for. I remember saying, "If you knew what I was struggling with, you would ask me to get up from this table and leave!" But Andy told me to go ahead and let them know how they could pray for me. I said, "I need help! I need prayer! I am struggling with pornography. I live by myself and I don't know how to stop. I tried to commit suicide in 1983 but couldn't go through with it. I told men at other churches and they said that all guys struggled with it and that I would be ok…or they told me the rules to follow." I was discouraged. I hated living alone. It made me feel worse. I was scared. My finances were out of control, even though I had never missed a rent payment. I was afraid I might try suicide again.

I looked around the table and saw compassion on everyone's face. Andy's eyes were moist.

After a few meetings, I asked Andy if I could help out around Open Door, and he had things I could do, so for the next five years, I never left. (And we had some really cool Bible studies.)

CHAPTER 25
Lessons of Helping

Also in 1993, a man named Wade Blank was supposed to dedicate the ramp at Open Door Fellowship. Wade was a pastor who worked at a nursing home. He saw that the disabled people at the nursing home were treated poorly so he filed a class action suit on their behalf and won! He helped disabled people, who might otherwise be looked on as a hardship on society, to become people of dignity and value. He also helped disabled persons maintain freedom within their own homes by learning to live inter-dependently. He started the Atlantis Communities.

Sadly, before he could dedicate the ramp, he died in an attempt to save his drowning son.

But the work he began lives on. My friend Carolyn Finnell was greatly impacted by the Atlantis Communities.

Some friends from the prayer group encouraged me to move into the Providence House. I kept telling them that they didn't want me there. But Andy encouraged me later and told me he could be my mentor! A mentor was required to complete the six-month to two-year program. I nearly jumped through the roof! (And we were standing on a parking lot, so how do you jump through the roof? But that's how excited I felt inside!) So I moved in in November of 1994.

I learned so much, like how to encourage those who wanted to leave the program. They were always welcome to come back. My friend, Jerry R., came close to leaving because he was failing with his addiction issues. Andy was mentor to both Jerry and me. Once Jerry called while I was meeting with Andy. He was telling Andy he wasn't going to make it in the program. Andy asked me to pray and to go for a ride with Jerry if Jerry asked. He did, and I went. Andy had told me not to give him advice, just to love him and listen.

Lesson Learned: This reminded me to step back from my problems and put my focus on the needs of others.

Jerry and I drove to the mountains. He stopped the car, walked around it, and smoked a cigarette. I began praying for peace for Jerry and wisdom and empathy for me. Then Jerry began to vent and share his feelings. I just sat quietly and listened and felt honored that Jerry was trusting me.

Afterwards, Andy encouraged Jerry to go to the Passion Play, which he did on several successive nights. Jerry tasted God experientially and saw that the Lord was good. Psalm 34:8

Jerry and I went on to work at Whiz Kids together, with Carrie and Bruce Duwell. Whiz Kids is a homework and Bible reading program for youth. Near the end of his time at Providence House, he was heading out for a date. I was leaving with my mom to celebrate my birthday and he hugged me and told me he loved me. I didn't know that would be the last time I would ever see him. That night he died in his sleep watching a movie at his girlfriend's house. Discipleship is indeed a life for a life.

I dedicate this story to Jerry's daughter.

Jody W. was my first roommate at Providence House. He was a great guy with a heart of gold. He was a terrific artist who loved to paint, much like my friend Silvia Molina and also my mom! They are all a reflection of our Lord who paints the skies, the waters, the mountains. He is the painter of every life in relationship to intelligent design. He is waiting and has opened the door of possibility for every human to spend eternity with Him! Humans are the highest and most important of all His creation.

This was the kind of life that Jody displayed on the canvas of his life. We had so much in common (except sports). We loved to fix and eat amazing food. Sometimes, the kind chef at the Governor's Mansion across the street from the Providence House would leave food for us and Joy Osby, a sweet elderly lady, would prepare it.

We would watch old black and white films on TV together, like John Wayne westerns and World War II movies. We could both imitate John Wayne's voice (and sometimes we ran it into the ground).

While watching movies, Jody would often fall asleep because of the medication he took for bipolar disorder. He loved Jesus but struggled with feelings of worthlessness.

Medication can make trying to accomplish certain things more of a challenge, but making things easier for a short period of time can be a tool that helps people get stronger! Focus requires discipline. Discipline can be improved with practice. It takes discipline, for example, to overcome social and racial barriers. First, we must expose them to the light. Then we must be willing to change, which is hard when our beliefs come from something we've observed or been taught. But change is possible if we are willing.

If you grew up in a home with harsh discipline, you have a tendency to be more fearful and cautious around others who are different from you. But the more I wanted to change, I became more open to people, foods, cultures, and ideas outside of my own. Jody and I had similar experiences and backgrounds. We encouraged each other and saw progress in our lives.

Once, Jody gave me a birthday card with Hebrews 12:13 on it. It said, "Make straight paths for your feet so that the lame may not be disabled, but rather healed." This verse has several connotations for me.

1.   Going off the straight path is a form of disobedience.
2.   Making straight paths is the idea of letting strength be built up before taking a more difficult route, such as climbing the stairs.
3.   The verse also spoke to me about racial reconciliation. God does not see color in the same sense we do. He sees us as a people of equal value.

Jody also bought me a ticket to a conference where Joni Eareckson Tada spoke. What a beautiful gift it turned out to be!

Derek Peterson was another roommate at Providence House (and later at Cornerstone Home). He was very loving, tenderhearted, and compassionate. He suffered from schizophrenia, but if I went to a sporting event and came home late, he would sleep in my bed until I came home, help me get undressed, turn out the light, and cover me with a blanket. He did this for several years! He didn't have any problem with it at all. He was always willing to help.

Once Derek and I went to a fireworks show. I asked him if the fireworks startled him or triggered past traumas related to his schizophrenia. He said yes, so I asked how I could help. He said, "If I get up and look like I'm about to walk off somewhere, grab my hand and don't let me go." That's what we did and it worked.

Lesson Learned: It's important to remember that we need each other. When someone is letting us know how we can help them, we need to be prepared to respond, especially if we are the one who asked how we could help in the first place.

CHAPTER 26
Lessons of Leadership

I've mentioned Carolyn Finnell several times. Here's more about my dear friend. She was very others-oriented. Not only was she in a wheelchair, but she also had a speech impediment, so she was extremely careful to protect other speakers. She had a deep trust in Jesus, who blessed her with practical wisdom. If anyone made her mad, she was quick to show it, but also quick to forgive if they admitted their mistake, even if she had been wounded or wronged. She was a gifted Bible study leader, along with Bruce, Jim Cessna, and Bill Merritt.

In the beginning, there was no money for TRYAD at Open Door. (TRYAD later became a ministry under Open Door Ministries, but this wasn't until 1997.) So I talked Carolyn into crushing pop cans as a fundraiser so we could have lunch when we got together for Tuesday prayer group. She brought the idea to the group and they liked it. People started bringing bags filled with pop cans to the TRYAD House, now called the Antioch House. (Eventually it grew too small for all the wheelchair users, crutch-walkers, and those who used white canes, so we moved into the Open Door sanctuary.)

We bought a battery-operated can crusher but it ultimately broke. Then I purchased a wall-mounted crusher which proved reliable. That can crusher from 24 years ago is still mounted in the room I call my office. Wow! We generated $35-75 each trip to the recycling center, which provided pizza and soda for our gatherings. As I crushed the cans I would listen to sports radio or the Christian station.

At this time, I was the TRYAD director and Carolyn was co-director. But as time went on, many TRYAD members became disgruntled and sad because I wasn't open to their ideas. I began to see that I was losing the group because I wouldn't listen to them. I didn't understand how or why their ideas were important if I was the person in charge. (In the same way, I wanted God to listen to me, yet God was waiting for me to listen to Him.)

So I decided to quit, but I didn't tell anyone, not even Carolyn. I just locked the door to my room at the Providence House, trying to make people think I was at the office, and I stayed hidden under the bed covers, depressed, sad, and mad, for several days. If I fooled anybody, it wasn't for long and I certainly wasn't pulling the wool over God's eyes.

The director of the Providence House, Kevin Grenier, told me he wanted to speak with me. The requirement to live at the Providence House was to work or volunteer twenty hours a week, and I was dropping the ball. He informed me that I needed to take donated bagels over to Christ Body Ministries. In a childish way, my pride was wounded because I didn't see this as meaningful work. Besides, I didn't have a good way to drag the bagels behind my wheelchair without the bag ripping. He told me he knew I could figure it out. He also told me that had I been in the military, I would need to obey the commander even if I disagreed with his decisions. I knew he had me there. Checkmate!

I responded that had I protested this assignment, I would probably be given the task of scrubbing the bathroom with a toothbrush. He quietly said, "I don't think you're too far from the truth there." He said I need to take the bagels or I could plan on moving out.

Lesson Learned: It is so easy to forget who is in charge, me with what I want, or God with what He requires, which is to love the Lord with all your heart, soul, mind, and strength. Mark 12:30

I bought a military style duffle bag, put the bagels inside, and hauled them down to Christ Body Ministries. I thought it was a demeaning job, but I was pleasantly surprised. They were so grateful! The way I had felt quickly melted away. I told them about the poor attitude I had had in my heart and I wept. The leaders thanked me for my honest confession and gave me a hug. I ended up taking the bagels three or four times before I told our leaders I was going to return to TRYAD.

I was so nervous to return, but when I did return I was met with a loving response. Carolyn was now the director. I met with her privately and asked her to forgive me, and without a word, she did her best to bring her wheelchair beside me and press her head against my chest. Her actions spoke louder than words. And three weeks later, she asked me to be her co-director. We prayed. She said "please." And I said "yes." The flame of our friendship was re-ignited.

My leadership style had been to tell people what to do. Carolyn instructed me in the way of servant leadership. God asked me to let Him guide me and let Him lead THROUGH me. He's never given up on me. To this day, I'm still the co-director of TRYAD and it is an honor.

Lesson Learned: In reading the story of the love between King David and his friend Jonathan, I'm reminded of the brothers and sisters in Christ who have so deeply touched my life. At the top of the list is my Lord and Savior Jesus Christ. Carolyn Finnell is in my top five.

Carolyn was a woman I could have married if she wasn't already old enough to be my mother! But oh, what a friendship we had. She taught others how to have fun, to be simple and childlike. One Saturday a month we would all travel to downtown Englewood to celebrate the birthdays of the month. On one such occasion, at Country Buffet, Carolyn noticed a serving tray with 24 individual servings of Jell-o. She began to move the tray back and forth to cause the Jell-O to wiggle and started laughing uncontrollably. Then the staff started laughing uncontrollably. But then a supervisor, who must have been having a bad day said, "Will you guys grow up?" To which Carolyn replied, "We are!" Then the whole restaurant erupted in laughter! Somehow Carolyn had quieted a modern-day Pharisee with very few words.

The next time we returned to the Country Buffet, the staff joyfully brought the story back up, but we learned that the supervisor was no longer there. Carolyn was sad because she thought maybe she had caused the job loss, but the new manager assured her that she had quit on her own. Then she assured us that we could wiggle all the Jell-O we wanted under one condition—that the staff could be included in on the fun!

Once, Carolyn and I were discussing something about TRYAD on the phone. We started to disagree, then became very angry, but Carolyn threw a humorous curveball. She said, "We better stop fighting, or someone from your house or mine might walk in and think we're married!" I started laughing so hard, my stomach hurt, and she was laughing just as hard. Then after a few moments of silence, I began to cry. Then she began to cry. We tried to remember what made us so angry. We were able to pinpoint the disagreement but not what made us so angry. We were able, at that point, to find common ground and peace after we prayed together.

Another time at Country Buffet, Carolyn took a drink from her glass with her straw and suddenly her false teeth fell into the glass. We all looked at her and felt bad, but she started laughing hysterically, with the straw still in her mouth and a steady stream of soda pop exiting the end of the straw! Finally, the straw fell out of mouth, but when she noticed the false teeth in the glass looking up at her, she started laughing all over again!

Lesson Learned: Carolyn's actions made me wonder, "Did Jesus find a way to make his disciples laugh, to break the tension of spiritual warfare?" Learn to laugh at your own mistakes. You never know, spiritual warfare may be broken.

Carolyn told me about how the Atlantis Communities took on our local busses. She was part of the Architectural Barrier committee relating to public transportation. An action took place whereby Atlantis people blocked the busses by chaining their wheelchairs together. Some of those in wheelchairs were arrested, but when it was discovered that the jail cells were not wheelchair accessible, the protestors were told they were free to go. And where did they go? They made a bee line right back to where they had been protesting, at Colfax and Broadway in the heart of downtown Denver!

On a similar note, my mom was very involved in the Governor's Committee for the Handicapped. She helped in getting the earliest version of architectural barriers addressed, such as sidewalk curb cuts, which helped not only the disabled but also anyone transporting a baby in a stroller. She also helped set up a painting contest regarding how architectural barriers keep people away from opportunities to serve their local governments. The winner won a college scholarship. Mom took me to some of these activities. She told me, "I want you to learn to advocate for yourself, because someday I'll be too old to do that for you."

Lesson Learned: There's a time and place for going through the normal processes for change, but sometimes, people don't listen. My mom wanted me to be a teacher to others. Carolyn taught me the importance of civil protest and that sometimes we must take extreme action. As it turns out, after the action, the busses installed lifts for wheelchairs and other adaptive equipment. There's room for both—civil protest AND being a teacher to advocate for yourself and others.

Carolyn helped me learn the value of listening to each other, especially when the rights of those unable to speak for themselves were trampled on. (For example, I disagree with abortion except when a woman has to choose between her life and her child's. The unborn are unable to speak for themselves.) And I disagree with resistance to arrest if the police officer is just doing his/her job. The officer might be a Christian and may very well empathize with the protestor, yet he/she has a job to do, by the very taxes we pay and the Constitution as well.

Fortunately, there was victory through the Americans with Disabilities Act of 1990. Reconciliation between estranged parties began to take place.

CHAPTER 27
Lessons of Diligence

In the mid-1990s I took a class at the Community College of Denver to learn how to use Windows voice recognition software. The class and teacher were great. I worked very hard in the classroom day after day. The professor frequently encouraged me to take breaks, but I was so eager to learn. He was serious though, because he felt I was trying too hard and not being patient with myself. At one point he said, "One of these days, if you don't take a break, don't be surprised if you start to feel your wheelchair rolling outside. If I have to, I will push you outside with me while I take a smoking break. You are a great student, but you are working your fingers and your mind to the bone!"

Well, a few days later, that's exactly what happened. There I was, sitting outside next to him during his smoke break. Before he lit his cigarette, he looked into my eyes and said, "Take a break and get some fresh air. Sometimes the computer may not be responding to your voice the way you want it to, because you're tired and frustrated! You are doing fine, Randy, but please take a break once in a while for your own well-being. If every student I had worked as hard as you, they would all make straight A's."

I did make an A in his class! But I still had a lot to learn!

Lesson Learned: Don't be hard-headed. Listen to your mentors, teachers, and professors! "Those who have ears, let them hear!" Matthew 13:43

In 1995, Lana was injured in an accident and was in significant pain. She had three injured vertebrae. I had been telling her about *You Gotta Keep Dancin'* by Tim Hansel (regarding her pain). The very next day, a friend dropped that book off at her home without knowing of our conversation! (Lana now has serious vertigo and needs our prayers. She is one of my favorite people. Her faith is very strong. She knows God uses suffering to make us stronger.)

Lessons Learned from the Bottom of the Stairs

In 1996, I met Cliff Stein and quite a few other baseball lovers and it was like a honeymoon! I would sit in our new baseball stadium (Coors Field) with a relatively-new baseball team (the Colorado Rockies) with brand new friends! Cliff would pick me up at 4 p.m. and I would get home around 10 p.m., except on Friday and Saturday nights when it would be 11 p.m. because I was chasing autographs. In many ways, I lived at Coors Field when you calculate how many hours the home games took!

I learned from Cliff (and later from Danny Wood) about being respectful towards the players. Whether taking batting practice or shagging balls in the outfield, they are professionals. Yes, you might say they are adults playing a child's game, but they work hard and have serious responsibilities! I learned to ask for their autographs like this: "If you have a chance, can you sign a baseball for me when you get done working?" This was new for me. They weren't on the field for my self-gratification. I learned to enjoy the game more by remembering this perspective.

I learned to deeply appreciate the conversations, laughter, transparency, humility, and honesty from players. This compelled me to love, respect, and appreciate them even more.

As the years went by, these weren't just games any more. I was captivated by the drama, heartache, and celebration of hard-fought wins and disappointing losses. I could relate them to events in my own life—the exhilaration and the devastation. I also drew on World War II images and characterizations in movies such as *A League of Their Own*. I drew on events in the lives of friends, i.e., the real world. I realized there are people cheering for me in the present. Even saints that have gone on before are in heaven cheering, as if they are in a stadium watching me (and you) as life plays itself out. And God the Father, God the Son, and God the Holy Spirit, along with the angels, are pulling for me and pulling for you!

Lesson Learned: See the Faith Hall of Fame chapter, Hebrews 11.

In 1998, I had the great pleasure of enjoying the first and biggest Super Bowl Bronco victory with Andy's family. The anticipation was high! The Broncos had taken so many beatings in four previous Super Bowls beginning in 1977. The Broncos were playing the Green Bay Packers. At first, the Packers went down the field like a knife through butter. (Oh no, not again!) But the Broncos came back. It was a real dog fight. Near the end of the game, John Elway made a spinning helicopter dive for a first down. He jumped up and threw his fists in the air! The Broncos took the lead 31-24. The Packers tried to score but we stopped them and won.

A few months later I went to a Rockies game and found out that the Broncos were going to make a guest appearance to be honored by the Rockies. I sat in the tunnel leading to the basement where the Broncos were likely to be, hoping for an autograph or two. The head Rockies representative told me, "There will be no conversations with the players because Mike Shanahan (the coach) said no autographs!" So I replied, "May I speak to them if they speak to me first?" (I had a plan.) He said yes.

As Alfred Williams came out, I smiled and waved but didn't speak. And he said, "Hey there, how are you?" So I asked him to sign my Super Bowl 32 football. Then I asked him if Terrell Davis could sign the football. (Terrell Davis was the game's MVP.) Terrell did. I now had these two autographs as well as Mike Shanahan's on my football. Mike Shanahan had told me personally two weeks earlier that he does not discourage his players from signing autographs.

(Thank you, Cliff! Seat 17 paid off again!)

But the Rockies representative was mad and called me a blankety-blank spoiled brat. The blanks were an uncalled-for reference to my disability. I reported this to Rockies management and appropriate action was immediately taken.

By the time Super Bowl 33 rolled around, my sister Lana and her husband Brent (Brumfield) had moved to Pueblo, Colorado. I went there to watch the game.

And the Broncos won Super Bowl 50 with none other than Peyton Manning leading the charge. My nephew, Brooks Brumfield, called me to enjoy the moment. I love my nieces and nephews, Brooks,

Marshall, and Lauren. I love you too, Brent and Lana. And Brent's dad, James. James and I would joke about Colorado vs. Louisiana. Big C. Little l. ("Little L" is a fun poke at Louisiana.) May the peace of the Lord be with you all always.

Just after I graduated from the Providence House, receiving the coveted rubber ducky, but before I moved into Cornerstone Home, I learned an important leadership lesson. It had to do with the spiritual metaphor of mountain climbing. My brother, Robert, was a mountain climber as was one of my close friends, Tom M. (Tom was also my golfing buddy.)

Robert's greatest achievement that I remember was when he and three others climbed the Grand Tetons near Jackson, Wyoming in 1998. I was with my brother that day. He gave me the honor of leading the climbing team (including his sweetheart, who is now his wife, Diane Spalding) in prayer from the base with a microphone. They were making the climb that had been made 100 years earlier to the day. Robert's great-great uncle was arguably the first to reach the summit of the Owen-Spalding route 100 years earlier. I reflected on what I had learned about mountain climbing through Tim Hansel's book, *You Gotta Keep Dancin'*.

CHAPTER 28
Lessons of Humility

After that trip, I moved into the Cornerstone Home with my housemates, Derek, Donald G., and Fred Winter. Cornerstone is owned by Open Door Ministries. A big part of the vision and purpose of Cornerstone is to help each other and use each other's gifts and talents to compensate for each other's weaknesses.

Fred always enjoyed greeting people. And people were always glad to see him. He worked at Safeway. He would get very excited to tell you about the newest person he had met there! Fred passed away in 2010.

Kevin and Lisa Grenier gave those of us at Cornerstone a new dog, a German Shepherd/Labrador mix named Mario. Mario was a great dog. He destroyed the couch due to separation anxiety, but he was a great dog. I had him neutered, which calmed him down, and took him on long walks. The veterinarian suggested that I become his primary master since I was with him the most. Later, due to my move out of Cornerstone, I had to send Mario to live with my sister, Brenda, in Michigan and he was happy and became bigger and stronger. He recognized my voice over the phone! He would speak when I said, "Mario, good dog! Speak!"

Then, when their electric fence broke, he got away and was hit and killed by a car. After working through the grieving process, Brenda and her daughter, Rachel, went looking for a new dog in the month of June. They found one and named her June.

And then, Brenda and Rachel moved from Michigan back to Colorado, so I got to visit them (and June!). My legs and feet were swollen because of water retention. Brenda lovingly cared for my feet, and amazingly, so did June! June would lay her head across my wounded feet and lick them. When I smiled at her, she would wag her tail. It's almost as if June was an angel in four-legged form. My family loves dogs. And we can learn life lessons from our four-legged friends.

Lesson Learned: God provides laughter, comfort, and encouragement through our four-legged friends.

When I started living at Cornerstone Home, I thought I would go to a clinic closest to my home since it was less than a block away. It's called East Side Health Clinic. I inquired about getting a power wheelchair there, because I was experiencing aches and pains due to cerebral palsy. They didn't bother to ask why I thought it was important to get a power wheelchair. They just told me they wouldn't help me get one simply so I could have a toy to play with! I considered that insulting because I was raised to think and be smart and to advocate for myself. The doctors at the ICHC had continued to help me learn more about advocating for myself and others. My co-workers who served on the ICHC Patient Advocacy Board and I developed this phrase: "Your doctor. Your dignity." The doctors, patients, and staff strive to communicate this and live it out at ICHC. The people at the East Side Health Clinic assumed, without exploring the truth, that I was interested in an electric wheelchair as a toy!

When I walked out of that Clinic, the first person that came to mind was Bob Williams and the ICHC. In the end, he helped me get my first power wheelchair. (I have not received any help from any other Colorado medical institutions unless absolutely necessary. And sometimes it has been necessary.)

Although I moved into Cornerstone Home in 1998, due to my pride and impulsivity, I moved back out in 1999. (Among other things, I had struggled with the house being painted baby blue. "Baby blue is for sissies," I thought.) Andy had warned me that if I ever lived alone again, more than likely I would return to my old bad habits like a dog returns to its vomit. Proverbs 26:11 and 2 Peter 2:22. And that's exactly what happened.

I had struggled with learning how to live with my roommates. (The one who had the biggest problem was me.) But alone, I struggled with having to push my manual wheelchair on flagstone sidewalks. I struggled with grocery shopping. I struggled with loneliness.

Lesson Learned: The truth is, I was feeling insecure and inadequate about my disability. I had spent so much time running away from these feelings, but I wasn't aware of that, because to me it was normal. I may have learned some of this from my father, but somewhere along the line if you learn something from someone, but then choose to practice it, it isn't their problem any more. It's yours. If you can relate.

CHAPTER 29
Lessons of Love

It was during this period that I took a job using some of the skills I had learned at the Community College of Denver. My friend, Debbie Johnson, while working at the company she started called DenverWorks, looked into various employment opportunities for me, along with my vocational rehabilitation counselors. I finally found an opportunity with Big Brothers Big Sisters in telephone marketing.

But the voice recognition software didn't work. There was no problem with it. The actual problem was the size of the office! There were somewhere between 8 and 10 co-workers crammed together in a very confined space. When I tried to give commands to my computer, the computer picked up not only my voice but also the voices of several co-workers, all at the same time. The computer was printing on my screen whatever it thought it heard. I ended up using a few fingers to do the job I thought my school training would provide.

I met Mark L. there. Mark was bright and insightful and loved to laugh. We both loved baseball. He was from Baltimore and loved crab cakes…and the Baltimore Orioles baseball team, especially the player Brooks Robinson. Brooks had come to visit him in school and got right down on the floor with the students!

Not long after that I learned that Mark was a Christian. Before I met him, my favorite Christian from Baltimore was Joni Eareckson Tada. What do the two of them have in common? They both love Jesus Christ and both are disabled. Joni is a quadriplegic and Mark is blind.

Mark's wife, Peggy, is also blind. Once I went and stayed at their apartment. We discovered a mutual love for country music, and later went to a Randy Travis concert together. Mark and Peggy even raised a child together. I really enjoy their friendship and the courage and perseverance displayed in their lives.

I worked at the Big Brothers Big Sisters call center for a couple of years. It was for booking appointments for donation pick-ups. Later, I worked at AON for six months. I got chewed out by the government for going over what I was allowed to make on SSDI by $1! They could have nicely informed me, but they chewed me out!

I'm done with jobs. I'm just allowing the US government to pay me for serving Jesus Christ!

I also met Heather Seaver at Big Brothers Big Sisters. Heather is also an incredible Christian woman who happens to be blind as well as epileptic. She loved music...and I found her very attractive and extremely intelligent. She had the ability to read with a monocular on the right side of her glasses. She would joyfully read out loud to me! She would read a chapter from the Bible or from *Fresh Wind, Fresh Fire* by Jim Cymbala when we arrived early at work and enjoyed an apple fritter together. I would pet her "seeing eye" dog, Jova.

We began dating almost immediately after getting to know each other. We went to The Cheesecake Factory once a week and shared a plate (because the portions were so large). We were making plans and thinking way into the future. But we, especially I, were going way too fast.

I was finding my identity in her rather than in Jesus Christ. I didn't know how to share my feelings with God very well. And I was struggling with understanding how to listen to Him and recognize His voice. My pride was in the mix.

I decided to sing in the church choir with her, and we also spent a lot of time at her parents' home. I had a lot of respect for her father, Donald Seaver. He wanted to know immediately where I stood in my relationship with Jesus Christ! He helped me use Velcro to stabilize my crutches in the crutch holder, so I could use my wheelchair like a car. On occasion, Heather and I would go to events together or hang out at my apartment. I would pay a cab driver to get her home safely. We spent Easter and Christmas together with her family.

One day, when her parents, Penny and Donald, went on vacation, I invited my brother Teddy over to Heather's house, so he could meet her. We had a good time but ate almost all the cream puffs in their refrigerator. I gave some money to Teddy to go to the store and buy more cream puffs to replace the ones we ate, but when Penny (who like all moms has eyes in the back of her head) returned, she knew the container we bought was not the same one she had bought. But thank you, Penny, for not being too hard on us! They were so good, but I was so embarrassed.

If Heather ever missed church, it was likely because she had had a seizure. I would send flowers home to her by her dad.

As our relationship continued to move fast, understandably, Penny and Donald became scared for their daughter and concerned for me. Donald had no anger towards me and told me that if it was the Lord's will for us to marry, he would get out of the way. This was not so easy for Penny to do. Looking back, my biggest regret was that I did not try harder to empathize with her in a more constructive way.

Heather and I began talking about living in a Christian Community Home. I thought that if I took every step I could think of to show her parents I was trying to be a responsible leader, it would help them relax, but in the end, I was making it more difficult for them. I was going too fast and not allowing the relationship to blossom naturally. Heather introduced me to one of her favorite pastors, Ralph Grosser. He could see that I was struggling to trust God. He told me that if it was God's will for this relationship to become a marriage, no human could tear it apart, but if it wasn't God's will, no one could put it together, not even me. He reminded me to be at peace with God's will concerning issues like this.

But as you will see, I still have a lot to learn on this matter. (More about Heather later.)

On April 20, 1999, I heard about the Columbine tragedy while at work at Big Brothers Big Sisters. I went to Coors Field for that night's baseball game, but it was cancelled. As I turned my wheelchair around and headed down the long dark hallway of the Coors Field basement, I saw my favorite Colorado Rockies player, Todd Helton. I remember the sound of his cleats tapping on the pavement with each step he took. I sped my wheelchair up to stroll beside him. We talked for a while, then walked side by side in silence for a bit, then I asked him, "I know today is a very bad day, but would you be willing to sign an autograph for me?" And he put his bags down and said, "That might be one of the better things I do today."

When I got home, I learned exactly how close the Columbine tragedy would touch me. I recognized the last name of one of the young shooters—Klebold. Dylan Klebold. His mother, Susan, was one of my Vocational Rehab counselors. I was very comfortable with her. She's a kind person. I was able to write a letter to her letting her know that I deeply appreciated the work she did for me and that I was sad for her over the loss of her son. I told her that God loves her and so did I, and that I would continue to keep her in prayer.

Lesson Learned: It was a privilege to have the opportunity to encourage someone like Susan in a very troubling time. 2 Corinthians 1:3-11, John 8:32.

I had moved into my apartment in 1999 and God chose to bless me relating to a prayer I had prayed in 1992. The prayer was this. I asked God if He would open a door for me to go to Alaska if I paid off my credit cards. I had wanted to go to Alaska previously on a sea kayak trip. I had asked Mom is she would go with me, but she declined saying she didn't want to sleep outside under mosquito nets! I ended up not going on that trip due to those debt problems. Here's how the second opportunity came about.

I went to Boulder to watch a University of Colorado vs. Oklahoma football game. A man tapped me on the shoulder and asked me to prove that the seat I was sitting in was indeed mine. Long story short, I was able to do so, and he said, "I'm with America West Airlines. If you'll allow us to flash a picture of you holding an America West Airlines sign on the Jumbotron, we'll give you two tickets anywhere America West flies." So I said yes…and the tickets were mine! I called my mom to see if she could go to Alaska with me and she said yes, provided I would sleep in a hotel room and not outside under mosquito nets!

In August of 2000, I went on the trip to Alaska with Mom. When we reached Alaska, we were able to stay in the home of my sister

Brenda's high school friend. Her name was Shawn. It was hard to keep my mind off Heather. It was hard to see where one life begins and another life ends. I was struggling to grasp how my life would go on if God was trying to tell me that Heather and I being married was not His plan.

Mom rented a car and we drove all around seeing beautiful flowers, unbelievable wildlife including eagles, Mt. McKinley, Resurrection Bay, and places where the ocean came up flush against the side of the Rocky Mountains. We ate in restaurants where the seafood was cheaper than we could have ever dreamed about. Some of the beauty made Mom and me cry like babies.

I had longed to see Alaska since my Southern Gables friend, John Meyer, read John Muir's book, *Notes on Alaska*, to me. I was now seeing some of the same things John Muir must have seen around the time he met Theodore Roosevelt.

The next day, Mom and I went deep sea fishing in Homer. I should say that I fished and Mom watched. I went fishing just for the halibut! Haha! I had found a company called Sorry Charlie's Fishing Expeditions that had experience anchoring a disabled person's wheelchair to the inside of the boat with ropes, then anchoring the person to the wheelchair. I was so excited to go! There were other passengers on the boat and some were pulling in fish that were 125 pounds or more. They had to strain and pull with their legs and backs to do so, but it was beautiful to see.

I was patient and it took some time before something took the bait on my line. Sadly, I could tell it was far less than 125 pounds, but the lactic acid had started building up in my arms and shoulders. I told God of my sadness and felt Him remind me about not having the use of my back and legs.

Lesson Learned: God had given me something I could handle. My fish weighed 70 pounds. The next one I caught weighed 30 pounds.

The staff on the boat had to shoot the halibut because they are so strong. Their tails could knock a person silly! The staff packed the fish and shipped them to Colorado. I thought it would take a while, so I called my brother and asked him to watch for their arrival. To my surprise, he said they had already arrived, and that he had to give away food in Mom's icebox because the halibut took up the whole icebox! Mom asked me to see if people from church or the Providence House could use some of the fish, because otherwise she would be eating halibut for breakfast, lunch, and dinner for the next year!

The next day we toured the rugged countryside, then the following day we took a sightseeing boat and saw puffins and an otter floating on her back with her baby on her stomach. What a blessing from the Lord. On the boat, I was thinking of Heather and began to cry, but then something amazing happened. The captain told us to look out the window at the whitecaps on the water. He told us it takes three days for whitecaps to disappear after a storm and for the sea to become completely quiet, even as the sun is shining. And the captain talked about Jesus telling the sea to be quiet—to the whole crowd on the boat! Jesus rebuked the wind and told the sea to be calm and still. Mark 4:39.

Mom went to the upper deck to take pictures of whales. I took this opportunity to share my feelings with the Lord. I asked Him to calm the storm in my heart. Then I fell asleep! After I woke up, and for the remainder of the day, my heart remained calm.

I later found the gift I wanted to give Heather. Mom knew I had found the right gift because I was clutching it to my chest and crying. When we returned from Alaska, I gave the gift to Heather and she was so grateful.

A week and a half later, we were together at one of our favorite spots, the Tattered Cover Bookstore. She calmly told me she didn't think we should date any more, that she didn't think it was going to work out. It took everything I had not to burst out in tears or lash out in anger. Surrender did not come easily, but I calmly turned away and made my way toward the front door. Just as I got to the door, she called out to me. I turned and she was crying on the outside like I was crying on the inside. She said, "I still want to be friends!" Then I told her I had never been able to do that very well after a breakup.

I told her that if we were going to be friends, we needed to pray together as often as possible for the next six weeks. We did. And we got stronger as friends. It wasn't easy. The transition wasn't perfect, but it was a miracle! She is one of the best friends I have in my life today and I know she would say the same.

Heather later married Bryan Reed. I was so thankful to attend their wedding. But before the wedding, I heard that Bryan would be attending a men's retreat in Glenwood Springs that I was also going to attend. I asked to share a room with him. I waited to be sure he was in the room before I went in. I said hello to him and he turned around, surprised to see me. He told me he felt bad. He felt like he had stolen my girlfriend away, but I was able to assure him that I didn't feel that way and that it wasn't God's will for Heather and me to be married.

Bryan has been helpful to me in many ways. We talk sports and laugh. We've even had several heart-to-heart discussions. I told him I wanted the best for Heather and for him and that I wanted to remain friends, but if he felt uncomfortable with that, I would respect his decision. Today, more than twenty years later, the three of us are still friends. To God be the glory!

CHAPTER 30
Lessons of Healthcare

After my breakup with Heather, I moved back into Cornerstone Home in 2000. I apologized to Derek and Fred for leaving so abruptly. Glen Westfall had been our house director, but now he had business and family commitments that meant he could no longer serve in that role. We soon got a new house director, Eric Davis.

As you can see, there have been many highs and lows in my life. God has shown me that He is master over all, the good and the bad. For example, I have had a bad habit of being anxious or worried about things. I know I'm not alone. So here is a practical homework assignment that the Holy Spirit gave me one day. First, I looked up the word "anxious" in the dictionary. One of the definitions is to be agitated, like the little instrument in some old washing machines called an agitator. When you lift the lid to watch the water in those old machines, you can see the water is troubled by the back and forth motion of the agitator. Try to picture what it looks like to God when we worry about something repeatedly without confessing it to Jesus. We are creating tiny tracks in our brains, which can and do result in injury that is self-inflicted. We cannot blame anyone else because we have control over what we choose to do and participate in. That is just one reason it is called sin!

Lesson Learned: We need to trust God rather than give in to the enticement of Satan.

A close friend throughout the early 2000's was Linda Collins. I began to eat lunch with some of the women at the home where she worked as well as other guests. I vicariously learned from a women's retreat she had led. She taught me that Christianity wasn't an American thing, i.e., it didn't originate in America. She helped me understand how special and unique it was for Jesus to call Jewish fishermen to His work! These men weren't just fishing to enjoy the sunshine, like the fishing I had known. They were fishing to feed their families and had a Jewish legalistic follow-the-law-by-the-book background. To follow Christ meant risking being an outcast. But the Holy Spirit moved them.

147

Linda cared about the sick. When our friend Carolyn was in the hospital, one day we wore reindeer ears made of cloth when we visited her. We got a smile out of her, but she was talking about going home, and she didn't mean back to her apartment. I started to cry. Then Carolyn started to cry and all the bells and whistles in her hospital room started going off signaling she was in distress. I felt terrible, but the nurse and Linda calmed us both down. Linda and I knew that would be the last time we would see her. Linda helped me grieve. See 2 Corinthians 1:3-11. Throughout my time at Open Door Fellowship, I have been comforted by Linda and also by Andy, Kevin, Carol Delcamp, and Brad Allen.

But back to the women's retreat. Even though I wasn't there (obviously), the women came back and shared the project they had created at the retreat. It was from the book of Joshua, about how God asked Joshua to take twelve large stones from the Jordan River to set as memorials, so we got small bags of polished stones and wrote two-word phrases or a scripture "address" on each. The purpose was to put your testimony on stones and keep them in a silver bucket. That way, if someone asked you about them, you could dump the stones out and use them as markers to share your testimony. If the person had a lot of time, you could share all twelve. If not, just a few, but the process is really cool, especially for people like me with a mild learning disability.

Lesson Learned: Some people can stand in front of a microphone to share their story in a 45-minute time frame. Others can use stones and a pen to "slay the dragon," so to speak.

Linda loved finding what would touch your heart the deepest, then massaging your heart with it, in much the same way someone who cares about you would massage your sore back, but she did it in a spiritual sense, allowing God's love to flow through her to touch someone else.

In a similar way to the way Linda touched my heart, many medical people have touched my life. I want to share a bit about them. First of all, I have learned that able-bodied people are just like the disabled. The ground is level at the cross of Christ. I learned this lesson when I first joined the ICHC Patient Advocacy Board. My desire to become part of the ICHC was due to family members and friends who influenced me to be assertive and proactive in taking care of myself (and looking out for the interests of others as well). This included other patients, doctors, nurses, counselors, and staff at a medical facility or through home care.

I slowly began a more proactive approach concerning my physical and spiritual health care through the guidance and vision of the ICHC co-founders, Bob and Jan Williams. Bob helped me stay on top of my physical health. Jan Williams was my first of many counselors. All of them have helped me, over a period of time, to uncover the lies I was telling myself as well as the lies I was believing about myself and my parents.

Each person at the ICHC has been terrific. The Center installed an elevator for people with physical disabilities like myself. The services are very affordable, which gave me high incentive to learn how to live without running from the pains of life. I want to thank Greg, who was also in a wheelchair and assisted with my counseling, as well as Janet Nelson and Margo Casey. I want to thank Dr. Claussen, with whom I have enjoyed many great conversations about God. His daughters helped with music at TRYAD retreats.

Dr. Robert Cutillo was instrumental in starting the Patient Advocacy Board. I had never shared so much with a doctor about Christ Jesus and about the gift of healing through suffering until I met and got to know Dr. Cutillo. I love you very much, buddy. Thank you for your personal insight! And thank you for the tremendous encouragement you have been to me.

My current doctor is Dr. Doug Fairbairn. All of these medical professionals, including Sue with whom I served on a mission trip to Mexico, have been important people in my life. I have been free to talk about how Jesus Christ was changing my attitude and heart about life as a disabled person. They have helped me realize how long I've been around!

I am also so grateful for the following people who have helped me medically.

Dr. Harry Hughes. His dedicated work gave me the opportunity to be a highly-accomplished disabled athlete, including being among the first Special Olympic athletes in the 1970's (in Colorado regional and state meets).

My mom, who worked briefly at a hospital and took care of me through all my surgeries at Children's Hospital. I had to learn to walk again after each one. She got me connected with Easter Seals and Sewell Rehabilitation Center for therapy.

My stepmother, Shirley. She was a dedicated Intensive Care Unit Nurse at Baton Rouge General. She found Dr. Frank McMains who was highly-skilled in assessing the status of my cerebral palsy. I think she was able to travel with him on trips to El Salvador. She taught me the importance of hygiene. And she taught me to fish, i.e., how to hold your mouth at a quarter pucker so the fish will take the bait! I'm grateful to her for the impact she had on my father in helping him take a hard look at sobriety. She was able to help get him into the chemical dependency unit of Baton Rouge General Hospital.

My sisters. Thank you, Lana, for your service to Jesus Christ. Thank you for your work as a Nurse Practitioner. Thank you for your prayers and encouragement. (And your children have blessed my life so much.) Thank you, Brenda, for all you are doing in the medical field and for your encouragement in my life and in the lives of others, especially in the life of your daughter, Rachel.

May the Lord Jesus Christ continue to develop the fruit He started in our family to empower so many to contribute to the medical field. What an honor to be part of this and what a beautiful tribute to Jesus Christ and the strength He gives us. He is truly our biggest cheerleader and friend forever. Amen.

Good healthcare is not just physical! My grandmother on my father's side, Emma Milliken, helped me in the emotional and spiritual healthcare sense. She worked as a nurse when I was very young at St. Luke's Presbyterian Hospital. I look forward to seeing her in heaven. And I hope to see her husband, the grandpa I was named after, in heaven too.

Lesson Learned: In thinking about my healthcare, I'm reminded of the book called *A Shepherd's Look at Psalm 23* by Phillip Keller. If a lamb was prone to straying, the shepherd would have to break its leg to keep it from straying. That way, it would be carried by the shepherd. I think about the casts that were on my legs when I was a child. Even then, God was drawing me to Himself, the Good Shepherd.

CHAPTER 31
Lessons of Heartbreak

On September 3, 2001, several of us from Open Door Fellowship got together to discuss trying out for a play called *Catacombs*. (The original catacombs were associated with the Roman Empire. They were human-made subterranean passageways for religious practice.) We would have met the following Monday night, September 10, to continue the talks, but the Broncos had a home game against the New York Giants. The next morning, September 11, like many people, I watched television in horror as the first and second planes crashed into the World Trade Center in New York City.

We held tryouts for the play the subsequent Monday, Sept. 17. We reflected on the events of the previous Tuesday morning, and the play took on a significant place in my heart. I kept thinking about the people who had lost their lives, including the firemen. And I felt bad for the NY Giants football team, wondering if any of their family members might have been injured, or died.

The play is about a group of modern-day Christians hiding from persecution in a church. They are offered a chance to renounce their faith in Jesus Christ. Those who renounced their faith got food and necessities. However, they had to take the mark of the beast. Those who did not renounce their faith were killed—men, women, and children. In the end, those who died for the sake of Jesus Christ were clothed in white robes to signify their presence with Jesus, in glory.

Lesson Learned: This was timely in light of Al-Qaeda and all that was happening in our nation and world. I had a sense God was trying to speak to me…and to our nation. God wants us to prepare our hearts for eternity and to count the cost of discipleship. Matthew 16:24-26.

In 2003, I met a man named Jim Morris. Here's the back story. You might remember the movie called *The Rookie*, which is about a little league coach that was challenged by his players to try out for Major League Baseball if they won the tournament. Well, the kids won, so their coach tried out for Major League Baseball and made it. That was Jim Morris.

A few months before that, I had been talking to my dad about him qualifying for golfing's Senior US Open. Dad was practicing to bring his game up to a qualifying level and found out that he was officially invited to participate in a qualifying tournament. He still had a lot of work ahead of him. He would have to finish in the top two to qualify for the Open. Not only that, but Dad was 65 years old and many, if not most, of the qualifiers competing against my dad were about 55 years old.

I wanted my dad to understand one thing and that is that I thought he was a good player and could compete with anyone. Plus, I thought it would be neat for him to experience some success in golf since he had been sober for quite a while, since 1979.

During the time that Dad was waiting for the qualifying tournament, I met Jim Morris at a local bookstore. I asked him to pray for my dad because he was trying to qualify for the Senior US Open. Jim Morris said, "I will pray for your dad and tell him I said good luck." Then he gave me a copy of the movie, *The Rookie*, to send to Dad.

Well, Dad didn't qualify for the Open after all, but in my mind, he still proved he could play. Out of a hundred or more players, my dad finished in the top 15. His heart was broken because he had a dream of his own; he wanted me to be there beside him riding in a golf cart at the Senior US Open. But it wasn't meant to be. Yet with all that my dad has overcome, in my heart he is among the very best!

Just before Easter of 2005, I joined Carolyn in a silent protest on the 16th Street Mall in downtown Denver on behalf of Terri Schiavo. Terri had suffered a heart attack that resulted in a massive brain injury. The protest was a joint effort between Atlantis Communities and our local transportation company, RTD. On the 16th Street Mall, the disabled persons were parked in front of a shuttle bus. A police officer asked the driver if we should be arrested and the driver said no, that this was arranged ahead of time. Carolyn and I has such joy in our eyes! We also had such joy as we saw the plaque at the end of the Mall (at Colfax & Broadway) that was a result of hard-pressed effort so that social change can remain effective and lasting.

This event caught the attention of the entire nation. Terri Schiavo's case divided the nation. Some saw it as a right-to-die issue. Carolyn and I and many other disabled persons saw it as a right-to-live issue.

By court order, Terri Schiavo's feeding tube was removed and she died on March 31, 2005.

Little did I know that Carolyn would herself go home to be with the Lord a year and three months later. She is buried at a site near the Mount Lindo cross. Because of her work in the community, she met the family that owned this land. But the truth is, only her earthly body is buried there. Her spirit rests in the presence of the Lord!

Lesson Learned: The same promise waits ahead for all of us who have put our faith in Jesus Christ, if we do not turn back.

This book I am writing is due to a dream she had. A few years after she died, I also had a dream…a dream to build a home for disabled women and men. Carolyn herself never lived in a community home. She had lived in a government-funded facility, but due to the work of Wade Blank and others on a class-action lawsuit, she was able to live independently with long-term care. However, both of us had a dream of community living for disabled men and women.

As I write this, I think about the glory of God that shone down on us on that day at the 16th Street Mall. I rejoice over Carolyn's life and the whole TRYAD ministry as I listen to one of my favorite worship songs called "Overflow" by Richie Furay. Thank you, Lord, for your blessings. May your love forevermore overflow!

CHAPTER 32
Lessons of Symbolism

When I first heard about Hurricane Katrina in August of 2005, that it was a category 5 storm in the Gulf of Mexico, and where it was headed, I was sad for my parents in Baton Rouge, which is just a couple of hours north of New Orleans. The storm was so big…and its eye so well-defined.

Hurricane Katrina caused Lake Pontchartrain, which is 338 miles from the Gulf, and Lake Maurepas, which is 344 miles from the Gulf, to back up. Lake Maurepas covers 93 square miles and is halfway between Baton Rouge and New Orleans. This resulted in catastrophic damage. I cried hard when I saw the devastation and I cried harder when I saw people whom I didn't even know, weeping.

I thought of my friends and family in Louisiana, people at Tara High School who helped me achieve my dream of a great high school experience—student government, Key Club, and participation in football, basketball, and baseball. They also helped me academically. They helped me achieve what people in special education school said was impossible!

I was determined, through my church, to find a way to give back to those who needed it, to those who gave to me. I thought the best way to give back and let them know how much I loved them was to organize a group of 9-12 people to go to New Orleans on my behalf. Among them were David, Brad, Peggy, Derek, Jennifer, Aaron, and others.

I wanted to bless them when they returned. I also wanted to bless the Castle Rock Church people in New Orleans for assisting them. I thank them all for being the arms and legs of Christ, who placed the vision on my heart. This was in the spring of 2006.

Lesson Learned: We can use symbols for communicating our thoughts and feelings. I wanted to bless the team with two symbolic flowers. (The flower image is from Songs of Songs 2:1. "I am the rose of Sharon and a lily of the valley." These are symbols of Christ. Christ has the strength of a man and the tenderness of a woman.) The sweet-smelling rose grows everywhere in the world and therefore represents everyone. Sharon was a place where the rose grew on the Mediterranean coastal plain. It was abundant with life. The lily of the valley is a humble and lowly picture. It is white, symbolizing purity, and humble because it bows its head.

Around 2006, Dad came to visit me. Since I was too heavy for him to put me into his truck, I asked him to use my spare wheelchair so we could go around together. We spent two days together, in wheelchairs. Before he got back in his truck to go home, I gave him a cross Mom had given me. I used to wear that cross about my neck every day. Giving him the cross hurt in a way because it meant so much to me. Even though my dad used to spank me when I cried, this time HE cried over that cross. He told me I'm the best Christian he's ever known.

Lesson Learned: Some things are well worth the sacrifice.

Remember my collection of 450+ autographed baseballs? Around this time, Andy preached a sermon series from the book, *The Purpose-Driven Life* by Rick Warren. I asked Andy if he thought God might be able to use me by sharing my faith with baseball players. Andy replied, "I don't know. Why don't you ask God?" Then we prayed together.

When I pursued autographs on baseballs, I asked the players if they knew Jesus as their personal savior, and if so, would they include the "address" of their favorite scripture on the Sweet Spot of the baseball. Here are a few stories:

The first and most significant is the story of a player named Mike. When I met him, he was a catcher for the San Francisco Giants. (He's recently been with St. Louis Cardinals.) But back in 2005 or 2006, when I was first wondering if God could use me in the lives of baseball players, I asked him if he would sign a baseball for me with his favorite Bible verse (because I had heard he was a Christian). He told me it was John 3:16. I asked him how he lived out his life to reflect John 3:16 on and off the baseball field. He said, "That's a good question. I'm not quite sure how to answer it and I want to think about it some more, but I just want to reflect Jesus Christ and what He's done for me in all I do." Then he asked me what my favorite Bible verse was. I said it was 2 Corinthians 1:3-11, which says that He comforts us in all our affliction so that we may be able to comfort those who are in any affliction with the comfort with which we ourselves are comforted by God.

He said, "I don't think I've ever seen that verse before. I have a Bible in my locker and I'll look it up." (I thought to myself in my doubt and insecurity, "Sure you will.") But sure enough, the next day as I was sitting in the same seat, he told me that he had looked it up and then said, "I can't tell you how much of a blessing it was to me!" He went on to tell me he had been going through some difficult times, which I later found out had to do with post-concussion syndrome. He asked me to keep sharing my faith with others!

The doubt and insecurity I experienced reminds me of another story about my doubt and insecurity. When I first met Joni Eareckson Tada in 1989, she asked me my name, and I politely smiled and said, "You wouldn't remember if I told you." She replied, "You'll never know unless you try." And the rest of that week, she called me by name.

Why is this important? It's because God used my life verse (that I got from both the Bible and Joni's book, *Secret Strength*) to encourage Mike.

Lesson Learned: Thank you, Lord, for the opportunities you have given me! Help me overcome my insecurities. Help me in my unbelief. Remind me of 1 Corinthians 1:27, which speaks of God using the weak things of the world to shame the strong and the foolish things of the world to shame the wise.

As you can see, I've had many opportunities to meet amazing people and participate in experiences and adventures. For example, my mom, my friend Landy, and I went to the opening ceremony of Denver International Airport. We saw British Red Arrows, the Canadian Snow Geese, the Blue Angels, military helicopters, and stealth bombers, to name a few. Mom pushed my wheelchair past a C-130 cargo plane, so I mentioned that I wished I could get on one of those planes. The military commander heard me, so he and some military personnel pushed me up inside the plane. What a dream! Then they told me, "We have bad news. It's too steep to get you back out of the plane." But then they said they were kidding. Haha!

And as a child, I participated in an Easter Egg Hunt for disabled children on the lawn of the State Capitol and had the opportunity to give flowers to Governor Love's wife!

Lesson Learned: God has used physical symbols in my life, from flowers to wheelchairs to baseballs, to express His spiritual truths.

CHAPTER 33
Lessons of Children

In 2006, when our beloved Carolyn Finnell was in the hospital, Linda Collins stepped in to help give TRYAD a boost, followed by Laura Shank, who took over and has become a very dear friend. Laura's mom had a background working with disabled children. Laura got to know Paul Sheppard and they got married! What a fun time his bachelor party was!

Paul started as a maintenance person for Open Door Ministries and worked with the Open Door youth. Laura also worked with the youth, so that's how they met! Paul then got a job working with Adams County supporting disabled adults. What a beautiful thing it has been to watch this young couple, both devoted to Jesus Christ and to disabled persons. Paul and I serve on the elder board together and I'm Laura's co-director at TRYAD.

Dan Foster and others are on the TRYAD steering committee. What a soldier and servant of the Lord Dan is! He kept a promise to his friend, David O'Brien, to start a TRYAD ministry in Denver, which took place in 1982 or sometime before that.

Laura and I spent two years going through theological lectures online. The in-depth study on the topic of biblical suffering (The Theology of Suffering) was brought together by two incredible organizations, Joni & Friends Ministries and Dallas Theological Seminary. The theology of suffering has become my favorite topic, because God teaches about healing through suffering.
See Psalm 119, the longest psalm in the Bible. The partnership Laura and I share is equal to the partnership I had with Carolyn!

I now get to play with, teach, and pray with their children, Aubree and Micah, by interacting with them in Sunday School, when they come to TRYAD, or when I go to their house. Last summer I got to play with them while their mom and dad made grilled cheese, bacon, lettuce, and tomato sandwiches for a picnic in the backyard of my home, Cornerstone.

I've been able to work with children through Sunday School at Bear Valley. I've also worked with children whose parents are in a divorce recovery workshop at Southern Gables, and additionally through Whiz Kids and at Open Door.

Lesson Learned: "Jesus said, 'Let the little children come to me, and do not hinder them, for the kingdom of heaven belongs to such as these.'" Matthew 19:14

Another favorite TRYAD memory has to do with Inner City Immersions, encouraged and supported through Jeff Johnsen of Mile High Ministries. This story involved Bruce Duell, Scott Dewey, Steve Thompson, Coni and Len (who eventually worked with First Baptist Church/Golden, CO, where I was able to preach), and sometimes Jeff, who I enjoy being around so much. (He and his family had a special bond with Carolyn.)

Various high school groups would come in for the Immersion, which included a visit to TRYAD. Typically, one or two would share their testimonies, then the fun began! My friend, Sam Andrews, who was at the time head of the Recreation Department at Craig Hospital, let us borrow some manual wheelchairs for our Disability Awareness project. We also borrowed white canes from organizations that supported the blind. One student would lead another who was blindfolded through an obstacle course. Sometimes the lead student would play a prank, and Carolyn and I wouldn't necessarily stop the pranks as long as everyone was careful! And then everyone switched partners to help the other eat. We would debrief the frustration, disappointment, or anger, and hopefully everyone was able to laugh. We would end in prayer.

Lesson Learned: Reiterating what I've learned from my friend and pastor, Andy, we need to feel in order to heal. These students were able to feel something of what disabled people feel.

Moving right along, in 2007, the Rockies won 21 of 22 games to end the season. They qualified for the World Series but came up short when they were swept by the Boston Red Sox four games to nothing. Nevertheless, here's what led up to that point.

162

Lessons of Children

The Rockies played a one-game playoff and it looked like they were going to lose, but in the bottom half of the last inning, they got several key hits and won the game. So many people were celebrating. Then we swept the Philadelphia Phillies! Next up, the Arizona Diamondbacks IN Arizona. My friend Dan, his 4-year-old daughter Emily, and I had the opportunity to drive there and were able to get playoff tickets!

However, my mom and her husband, Jerry Kauffman were on their way to visit me in Denver. I wanted to see my mom…and I wanted to go to the game. I talked to her about it and she said, "Go sweetheart! I understand this is a once-in-a-lifetime priority. Remember, I've known you since you were little. Your first girl is baseball!" Then I told her I loved her more than strawberries and she told me she loved me more than chocolate chip cookies.

We went to batting practice before the game and Emily got to meet Baxter, the Diamondback mascot. My chest was tight and I was so nervous about the game, but we won the first game! As we were going home, I got to carry cute little sleeping Emily in my arms, in my red power wheelchair. It was a wonderful feeling to have her sleepy little head against my chest. I loved giving Emily and later her brother, Ryan, rides in my wheelchair.

Lesson Learned: It's great to build bonds with children and teach that everyone is equal in the eyes of God. Building a foundation of encouragement builds a fortress of hope in the hearts of young people. Hebrews 10:24-25

A short time before the second game, we (mostly Dan) were interviewed by the Rocky Mountain News. (My stepfather used to work for them, but now the paper no longer exists.) The Rockies won game two!
We got back to Denver for game three and expectations were high. We got there early, and our gang, including Danny and Nettie Wood, ate dinner together at a makeshift table at Coors Field—the lid of a high-top trash can! The Rockies won the two games at Coors Field. The last catch was made by Todd Helton holding his glove high in the air like the Statue of Liberty. The Arizona player slid on his

stomach, trying to make it to first base in time, but to no avail. The Rockies were going to their first World Series!

Thank you, dear Lord Jesus! There are more important things in life than sports, no doubt about it, but you have blessed us all with a free will. Thank you for showing me about character and compassion from athletes who know you. I hope I get to see Lou Gehrig standing next to you someday!

When I was a child, I prayed that one day I would see my very own MLB team play in the World Series. There is a brick with my name on it behind second base near Gate E at Coors Field. It reads, "My childhood dream came true." (And so did my prayer.)

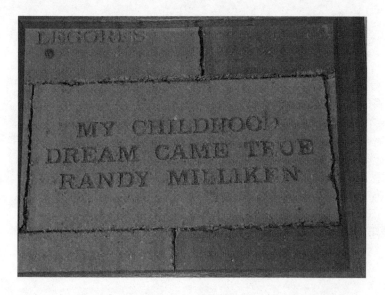

This section is dedicated to Dave Fleming with whom I built a special friendship at Coors Field beginning in 1996.

CHAPTER 34
Lessons of Community

Starting in 2005 and continuing until 2010, I was Eric Davis's assistant director at Cornerstone Home. In 2010, he got married and moved. I didn't want to become the director because I didn't know how, but God whispered this question into my conscience. "Would you let Me be director through you?" That seemed a whole lot easier, so I relaxed and let the Lord take over. I became the director in 2010.

Also in 2010, Mom's husband, Jerry, passed away. Because Mom had made me promise I would come back to the Catholic Church, I went to Holy Ghost Church with her at that time. We read through Psalm 23 together. I told her, "Mom, I'm back. I'm with God. I'm keeping my promise." Now she goes to church with me (at Open Door) occasionally when she's in town.

In 2011, when I was in the hospital after I had my gallbladder removed, my sister Lana came to assist me. I was very sick and didn't feel like talking. By nightfall the following night, Lana had been helping me non-stop. What a servant of the Lord she is! That second night, all I wanted to do was talk and talk and talk and all she wanted to do was sleep and sleep and sleep, so she politely began to read a book to me entitled *Shut the Blank Up and Go to Sleep*. Haha!

I've always appreciated the encouragement of my little sister Lana ("Tigger"), her husband Brent, my sister Brenda Frazer, my "Mother" Shirley Milliken, and my mom, Barbara Kauffman. I also appreciate my dad's mom, Emma Milliken, for the impact she had to get me going in the right direction with Jesus Christ.

Here's another memory from 2011. Andy once told me that he had gone to a St. Louis Cardinals baseball game and caught a baseball hit by the great Stan Musial (Stan the Man!). He put it in his lunch sack, took it home, put it on the table, and went to bed. The next morning, he went to retrieve it but the sack was gone! His mother hadn't known that a baseball was in there, so she threw it in the trash. As Andy ran outside to retrieve it from the trash bin, he saw the trash truck driving away.

When he told me this story in 1994, I told him that maybe I could help him get a new autographed baseball from Stan Musial! But I procrastinated and procrastinated. In 2011, I saw Stan Musial on TV making a guest appearance at a Texas Rangers and St. Louis Cardinals World Series game. He was 92 years old. I was glad to see that he was alive, but shocked and saddened as I remembered what I told had Andy I would do. So I got busy!

I called my friend, Danny Wood, who knew how to reach Stan Musial. Long story short, Danny helped me secure two autographed baseballs from Stan the Man, one for Andy and one for me. (In hindsight, I wish I had asked for a third signed baseball for Danny.) A few months later, Stan Musial passed away, but I discovered in an audiobook that he was a man of faith.

I was able to present the baseball to Andy at a neighborhood barbeque. He was like a kid in a candy store! People who enjoy sports have to have some little boy or girl still bubbling inside of them! Thank you, Lord, for the opportunity to share my faith and to encourage the faith of others.

I fondly remember the spring of 2013 when Michelle Warren was involved with the summer intern program. She delegated six interns to me for the disability awareness program. There were four sisters in Christ and two brothers in Christ. And what a great summer it was! I started off by asking them to watch the story of Joni Eareckson Tada with me to get a feel for how difficult it is to adjust to a physical disability, whether one is born with it or has a life-interrupting event. They learned through reflection and debriefing…and I learned something as well, about my denial through codependency. I am still unwrapping the gifts of wisdom I received through this program, like presents under the Christmas tree!

I created two-person teams for a ride on one of our light rail trains and a stroll down the 16th Street Mall. One intern would ride in my back-up power wheelchair and the other would walk alongside. They would observe the reactions of the people around them. Some would stare. Others couldn't care less. Still others might come up and say,

"I feel sorry for you." Then, the teammates would switch places, and later we would debrief.

I thank all six of the interns for what I was able to learn from the Lord through them. I am grateful to have gotten to know each of you! May the peace of Christ be with you always. And Michelle, thank you for your friendship and our partnership in Christ for the gospel!

Michelle exemplifies "community" to me. She has an incredible heart of empathy and compassion and has an enthusiastic passion for the Lord Jesus Christ! She currently works for the Christian Community Development Association. She was very supportive of my friend Carolyn and the whole disabled community, as well as the underprivileged community, people who lack the skills to advocate for themselves. I fondly remember when she took over as worship leader for Open Door Fellowship.

We at Open Door have a long tradition of what we call Share Sunday, which is the first Sunday of every month in which we share about how God is speaking to us. One particular Sunday, Michelle read from Psalm 107 where it says, "Let the redeemed of the Lord tell their story, those He redeemed from the foe, those he gathered from the lands, from east and west, from north and south." See also Nehemiah 1:1-8. Michelle goes out of her way to hear from those who have a praise story to tell or those who got caught in the teeth of a snare, broken and shattered, looking for encouragement to start over again.

She has a talent for gathering the worship team and congregation together for worship. And although the Holy Word of God says in Matthew 18:20 that wherever two or three or more are gathered in His name, there He is with them, we should never assume He is there, but should welcome Him with humility. He will not force Himself on us!

She frequently said to me, "He is the reason we are all here. I am only the donkey He is riding on!" At first I would laugh because of that funny image, but she said she was serious! And then I experienced the compassionate plea of the Holy Spirit for understanding and obedience, and my heart changed more and more.

I struggle at times to sing because I'm self-conscious about my voice, but beyond a shadow of a doubt, I love to hear music! I am deeply moved when lyrics resonate with my spirit, often to the point of tears. Music has always occupied a special place in my heart, predominantly through my childhood and teenage years, but also more recently. I was not blessed with a great singing voice but that hasn't stopped me in the love of music that I inherited from both my mother and my father. Music has touched me in a special way, mostly because I've loved love songs and because music has beckoned me to be introspective. Music was a tool that helped me to grow in my ability to express myself through poetry. However, I have learned that being introspective too much, too often, can have negative consequences at times as well. This would happen particularly if there was a young lady I was interested in. I would dream about the possibility of being in love when I listened to groups like Bread, Buffalo Springfield, Louisiana's Leroux, and so many others.

Yet after I gave my life to Jesus Christ, music became part of my joy. I have loved the music of Keith Green, Richie Furay, Glad, Amy Grant and many more. And I love the worship music at Open Door Fellowship.

Recently Michelle Warren and her husband, David, moved on to another church started through Open Door Ministries, Westside Church Internacional. David is the director of Open Door Ministries. He and the ministry have funded the publication of this book! They have been so supportive of this process and I'm deeply grateful.

Lesson Learned: Working with the interns and with Open Door Ministries has taught me so much about community. We each have a contribution to the kingdom of Christ. We're all part of the body of Christ.

CHAPTER 35
Lessons of Codependency

In 2014, Celebrate Recovery began at Open Door Fellowship. At that time, I became keenly aware of my struggle with codependency and my addiction to people. I have struggled with it for as far back as I can remember. I still don't have my ducks in a row regarding this matter. Yes, I handle it better, but it is still a stumbling block for me.

To me, codependency looks like:
*a deep feeling of insecurity
*deep worry about what others may think
*living vicariously through other people
*putting others on a pedestal and at the same time devaluing yourself (almost to the extent that you think of yourself as worthless).

I would put able-bodied men and women on a pedestal. It is a sign of how insecure and inadequate disabled people feel from time to time. I thought able-bodied people had better understandings of walking with God than I did. It is a lie because just like pride, it goes against what God says about how He sees/values us. When we do not value ourselves like God does, we are in effect calling God a liar. But when our views line up with God's view of us, we are freer to accomplish whatever He desires with the utmost confidence in Christ our Lord.

And finally,
*codependency is treating others as though they are a drug that you seek to put inside, so you can feel better about yourself. It is attempting to put other people into the god-shaped vacuum where only God belongs…putting the created thing in that space where only the Creator belongs.

As I worked through my codependency issues, I wrote this poem.

"Beauty in the Keyhole"
Standing in the doorway,
searching for keys;
Where is the answer?

Which one fits?
Heartache and longing torture me, like a thousand times before.

Standing at the doorway,
Searching for keys;
Where is the answer?
Which one fits?

A hated enemy,
A demon from the past,
Drops in uninvited,
Into the kitchen of my mind
And stirs a concoction of lies and half-truths.
It has an enticing aroma that clouds my thoughts and tears at my
confidence and self-esteem!

Standing at the doorway,
Searching for keys;
Where is the answer?
Which one fits?

Many keys seem to fit but only one unlocks the door.
That brings peace to quench the thirst of my soul.

Standing at the doorway,
Searching for keys;
Where is the answer?
Which one fits?

All of a sudden,
I feel trapped, as if my hands are tied,
As if my feet were bound.
The demon has done it again!

God has blessed me with a friendship and I raced ahead of him (all
without my noticing)
And I was tempted again to fill a longing
and tried to fit it into the god-shaped vacuum (my soul) where only
God belongs!

Lessons of Codependency

I was tempted and once again,
I fell in to a familiar trap of sin;
There are motives tied to events
From my past.
The ache from deep within urges me to try again.
It is insanity to repeat what has failed, to follow the same path and
expect a different result.

It was as if I were in a dungeon
A dark and lonely place,
Cold and damp

Standing at the doorway,
Searching for keys;
Where is the answer?
Which one fits?

This valley, this shadow of death,
Came upon me without a day passing, without the sun going down.
This demon came in, disguised in my thoughts, as light! As if he
were a friend greeting me with a handshake.
But before the night was over and before the cloud of his
concoction had lifted, he called out to me with laughter and jeers!
It felt as though he had stepped on my throat!

Now tears begin to flow as the floodgates slowly open,
Mingled with a sharp searing pain from the pit of my stomach!
While the light of my salvation, Jesus Christ, seems far off and
distant.
It seems as though He is nowhere to be found. Not because that is
the truth but because of lies and half-truths I am entangled with
and now mistakenly believe.

Standing at the doorway,
Searching for keys;
Where is the answer?
Which one fits?

Is it drugs? Is it drink?
Is it vicariously living through a version of my fellow man?

171

Even a brother or sister in Christ?
I have made the same mistake more times than I can count.
Even as I love our Lord and Savior Jesus Christ.

Why?

Standing at the doorway,
Searching for keys;
Where is the answer?
Which one fits?

One is correct,
All others are empty,
They lead in circles to nowhere.

Suddenly, I get a taste, a small sample of water I am looking for!
A water that will quench my thirst so that I will never thirst again.
Then, a nice man I do not know speaks to me. He says, "Hey! You
are smiling! You have a beautiful smile." But, since my confidence
and self-esteem have been low,
I do not know what to say.

I believed that my smile was ugly,
My smile was one of many things associated with my physical
appearance that I struggled with.
I did not want to say thank you in a hypocritical way, for something
I wasn't sure I was truly thankful for.

Then I remembered what the Lord said: In everything give thanks!
For this is the will of God in Christ Jesus for you. 1 Thessalonians
5:18.

Then I shouted at the top of my voice: "Praise the Lord!"
As I rolled down the 16th Street Mall.

Suddenly, a warm sensation came over me like an ocean wave in
the plains.
For the first time in a while, I felt the Lord wrap his arms around
me.

Lessons of Codependency

I gave the compliment that I struggled to receive, to the Lord. And He wrapped his arms around me!

Somehow, then I knew, this is only one of many answers from the Lord, that will help heal my confidence and my low self-esteem.

Then the Lord said: Randy you are loved!!! You are beautiful!!! You are a precious child. I created you! You are mine!

Standing in the doorway,
Searching for keys;
Where is the answer?
Which one fits?

Jesus is the key!
He is The Great I Am!
His love can sweep over us,
Like waves from the sea;
Binding our wounds and
Giving rest to our souls!

While working on my codependency with Andy, there were times he had to call to tell me we couldn't meet together on a specific Wednesday because something had come up or he had accidentally double-booked. When that happened, I would get depressed and feel my sense of self-worth drop. This happened many times.

But he would say with enthusiasm in his voice, "Hey Randy! Why don't you go talk to the students at the Denver Street School? Why don't you go speak in my place?" He did this several times over several years. His reasoning was so I would not keep my failure a secret. The Bible talks about exposing our dark ways to the light.

This helped me in a number of ways, including being dependent on the Lord rather than feeding my codependency on others. I saw the light! This makes me think of the song by that name that Jeff Johnsen would sing and play on his guitar. I used to dance to that song with Carolyn, spinning our wheelchairs in a circle!

Lesson Learned: You, Lord, have taught me lessons from great athletes, great books, and great people like Kent Matthews, Tim Hansel, Andy Cannon, Chris Hooper, and Len Billings, but the truth is they all came from you! Please help me to put you first before my fellow man. Exodus 20:2, Deuteronomy 5:6, John 14:9, and Hebrews 1:3.

Codependency reared its ugly head again recently when I went to the funeral of a friend. I had confessed it to the Lord, so I had been forgiven, yet I was feeling regret over the number of times I had been codependent in previous relationships. I was longing for the day, in heaven, when I know for sure that this repetitive sin would no longer visit me.

The beautiful thing is that I had been praying for God's help and He provided it. I needed to be able to press in to His Word and therefore press into Him. Sometimes people like me have longings they are trying to meet or want God to meet, but because of our motives, sometimes God says no, at least not today, and sometimes not ever, because that's not what His will is. He knows that in a prideful way we are trying to get our own needs met through our own devices.

Lesson Learned: Like pride, achievement can be our self-reliance, but God's desire is for us to turn to Him, not just for wisdom, but for nourishment that only He can give. Only He knows how to satisfy us with Himself.

For me, codependency was an addiction. I was addicted to people. Often, people think of addictions as substance-related. I have thought long and hard about that too. Years ago, many churches treated addiction issues as moral issues, rather than moral issues that have become addiction issues. Look at Romans 1:1-32.

Today at my church, groups like Alcoholics Anonymous, Celebrate Recovery, and other 12-Step programs treat addictions as they are, a disease. Yes, they are moral issues, but they are diseases, pathologies in many forms that damage the brain.

All of mankind struggles with the ultimate disease called sin, which originated with Adam and Eve when they ate from the tree of the knowledge of good and evil. Only the blood of Jesus Christ can cure sin, the original disease that we all have! I can only be honest here! Alcoholics Anonymous and similar 12-Step programs do not recognize Jesus Christ any more. They may have in the beginning, but they don't now, except to allow people to claim Jesus as their higher power. More and more, repeated references to the Lord and Savior are discouraged.

Celebrate Recovery takes the original Serenity Prayer and ties it together with other traditional aspects of the 12-Step program and includes scripture, while keeping the Lord Jesus Christ at the center! The Apostle Paul speaks for all Christians in Romans 7:19—"For the good that I want, I do not do, but I practice the very evil that I do not want." (NASB version). Celebrate Recovery goes on to provide recovery help through Christ.

Can the Big Book used in AA be helpful? I believe so! However, it cannot and will never replace the Bible. As Christians, through the power of the Holy Spirit inside us as we receive Jesus as Lord and Savior, we can understand and comprehend the Bible because it is spiritually-discerned through study and prayer. God wrote the Bible through men who chose to surrender to Him. The Bible is history and yet it is "His story" about the people He encountered and the lives He touched. It's not a textbook. The Big Book is closer to the definition of a textbook. The Big Book is helpful but should be kept as it is. It should not ever be substituted as an easier form of the Bible.

Lesson Learned: God will hold us accountable if we make that mistake. Don't touch the Bible. Not one word! The Bible is holy and sacred.

It is not my desire to judge anyone with these words, but we can rest assured that if we make the mistake of not giving the Bible its proper place, we risk being judged eternally if we do not turn back (repent) and do the right thing. Again, read the Big Book if you want to and I would encourage it, but keep the main thing the main thing. Keep the Bible first since God wrote it!

Lessons Learned from the Bottom of the Stairs

The Bible covers every issue in life including addictions. All of us as humans need only to turn to Christ Jesus for wisdom in the application of His word.

One of the ways my addictions started was through self-medicating. I dealt with my pain by trying to live vicariously as a player on a football, basketball, or baseball team. Starting in the mid-1980's, I transferred the practice of living vicariously to the girls depicted in pornography. The deeper I got into this, the more agonizing my pain became. And it would not leave me alone. I spent $14,000+ on it over time. This included purchasing Christian music in an attempt to ease my guilt and pain. But the guilt and pain came back up each time the next day, like a beach ball you try to hold under water, wishing it would just go away.

But thanks be to God! This addiction has now been conquered through Christ Jesus my Lord!

Lesson Learned: As you can see, God, in His mercy and power, has saved me in more ways than one and that's what sanctification is all about.

CHAPTER 36
Lessons of Prayer

In 2015, the elevator at Open Door was installed. It captures Open Door's philosophy. At first it seemed it would only go to the second floor rather than all the way to the third. I got upset. Yes, we are not supposed to worry and are supposed to trust the Lord, but I am admitting that I was worried. I was told the reason was cost. My worry and disappointment built into anger. This happened as I was driving my wheelchair home from a meeting about this issue. As I drove into my bedroom, I began to cry. It wasn't fair! I had had to fight for so much when I was young. I was allowing myself to be deceived by Satan because I was concluding that David Warren's words were final.

I began to pray, crying out to God. I said to Him, "This is your church. You say in your word that all of us are equal. Please help me, Lord Jesus! Help me to calm down and see things from your perspective! Help me to be patient with you and with those who love me!"

I told the leadership that God owns the cattle on a thousand hills, and that if the elevator didn't go all the way to the third floor, it would be sending a message to the disabled community that they were only welcome in part of the church.

Several days later, I drove back down to Open Door Fellowship and went inside. Within minutes I felt someone's hand touch my shoulder. When I looked up, it was David and he said with a smile on his face, "I think we can take the elevator to the third floor!" As it turned out, the money came in and the elevator sends this message— you are ALL welcome here!

I was so excited! It's hard to describe how I felt. I was so grateful that the Lord heard my prayer. It resonated through my heart and soul. My initial disappointment was probably related to the fact that I had struggled throughout my life, believing that my thoughts and feelings were not important to people, especially to other men.

Lesson Learned: Be patient with others in the church body, brothers and sisters alike, but especially with your brothers since trusting them is the most difficult! "Wait on the Lord." Isaiah 40:31. "Be slow to anger. Do not be anxious." Philippians 4:6-7

Soon the fundraising process started. We did all-night prayer because the fundraising process had become stuck. We confessed personal sins. We prayed for each other, then we prayed for the leaders in our church and for the residents of the homes. We prayed for the leaders of our city and federal government and asked God to hear us and forgive our sin. We prayed for everyone far and wide. We asked God to forgive those He has called out for His name's sake.

Not long after that all-night prayer experience, the floodgates opened. The finances we needed began to flow in.

There was another time during the fundraising process that we felt stuck again, so I asked David if we could do all-night prayer again. He said, "I don't have the time to organize it again, but if you are willing to organize it, I'll be there!" As I look back on this today, I can see another example of how the Lord was helping me to trust Him and trust my brothers in Christ even more. So I organized all-night prayer using the same outline David had worked with the Lord to create for the first all-night prayer meeting for the Family Room. The Lord heard our prayer again. The money we needed came together under the sovereign timing of the Lord Jesus Christ!

I can still use your prayers regarding my own prayer life today, but what I learned from these two experiences of all-night prayer (learned originally at Bear Valley Baptist Church as a member of Navigators) was deep and profound! God is so good! I recently was able to lead a third all-night prayer service at Westside Church Internacional.

When the construction process started, we had two morning services. The leaders decided it would be easier for most of the disabled people to attend the 11:15 a.m. service by a streamed process over television at the Antioch House, located across the street from the church. But I decided I wanted to set an example of love and empathy for the poorest of the poor, so I decided to attend both morning services, which meant traveling from my home through the cold and snow, as long as it was not so deep that it would prevent me from driving my wheelchair. Because of the faithfulness of the Lord, I was able to attend both services over 90% of the time.

But I would also discover that the darkness of my pride would be exposed. For many of the years that I attended Open Door Fellowship beginning in 1993, I thought I was better than the poorest of the poor. I thought to myself that they had put themselves in the position of sleeping out on the streets. I thought, "You get yourself out of the mess you are in. I'm not as bad off as you!"

Fortunately, my heart began to change because of the kindness of the Lord who bathed my heart in light for cleansing purposes. I'm not proud today of the attitude I had, but that's where I was, and that's what makes God's love all the more amazing!

Lesson Learned: He is a longsuffering God who is patient with us in all our afflictions! Romans 5:3 and 2 Corinthians 4:17 and 5:17.

During the construction process, some people entered the church through a doorway near the front yet off to the side. Others, including myself, would enter at the back of the church. The closest I could come to being in the sanctuary (until the Family Room project was finished) would be to park my wheelchair at the landing area in front of the stairs. This meant that people coming through the back of the church to get up into the sanctuary would have to step around and sometimes over my feet in order to ascend the stairs. If they came back down the stairs to take a phone call without disturbing the sermon, they would have to do the same thing to get back outside. The more I attended the first service, the more I realized that the street people were doing this.

Several weeks went by and it continued to happen. On one particular occasion, James V. Junior (I will call him) who was friendly to me and whom I had known for many years, was making these trips down the stairs and around or over my feet, so I prayed about how to handle it. The next time I saw James I asked him, "Do you know how much the Lord Jesus loves you?" He answered me with a loving but curious tone, "Yes, I think so!" So I said to him, "The next time you go upstairs would you look at the clock and ask God to give you the ability to stay upstairs and listen to the Lord speak through Pastor Andy?" He said sure. Then I said, "Good. I will pray for you too! And don't worry if you fail and don't stay upstairs very long. Remember, I love you but Jesus loves you more, so I will continue to pray for you and I won't get mad if you fail. Just pray to the Lord each time and He will give you strength to do your best for Him, okay?" He agreed and said okay.

As a result, over a period of time, James began to stay upstairs longer and longer to hear the sermon. I learned a lesson from this too! I learned that I wasn't so different from those I thought I was better than. I began to remember that in special education school I struggled with attention deficit problems. Frequently, my attention span was short in the classroom. It dawned on me that these brothers and sisters who lived and slept outside were not so different from me after all!

Lesson Learned: I'm not better than the poorest of the poor and I'm not better than my disabled brothers and sisters. We are all equal.

There's a song that I remember from childhood. One line goes like this, "Whoops, there goes another rubber tree plant!" My pride is like that rubber tree. When it gets exposed and brought out of the darkness by the Holy Light of the Lord, I can sing, "Whoops, there goes another rubber tree plant!"

Through the wisdom, love, and patience of the Lord Jesus Christ, God the Father and His Son win every time! All of us humans have a lot in common if we will just look a little deeper! We don't have to condemn ourselves. After all, that's what Satan wants! All we have to do is admit and confess the truth and the truth will set us free. Then we will be free indeed! John 8:32-33. This story about James V. Jr. is what inspired the title of this book.
Thank You, Jesus, and thanks to each person who was patient enough to step over and/or around my feet and not on them, which I would deserve if not for God's grace and mercy!

Lesson Learned: "Oh, the Lord is good to me. He gives to me the things I need, the sun and the rain and the apple seed! The Lord is good to me!" Amen.

CHAPTER 37
Lessons of Victory

God has blessed me with many opportunities to confront my fears and overcome them, yet I am still learning more about this every day! No, I have not yet arrived at perfection. Sometimes people think that if you overcome enough of your fears, then the rest of your walk with God will be easy. I have thought that way myself from time to time.

One of my favorite movies is *Facing the Giants*. When I first saw this movie, I was greatly moved and challenged. Later, because of it, I had an opportunity to give back and bless someone else, the Troy University Trojans.

I found out several years back that the Trojans were coming to Denver to play the Denver University Pioneers in basketball. I was told that they might be bringing me a gift. I had learned about Troy through my friend, Brad Allen, his father, Richard, and his brother, who played college football for Troy and then later, briefly, for the New York Giants in the NFL.

Sure enough, after the basketball game was over, the head coach, Don Maestri, and his team gave me a Troy basketball t-shirt. I thought this was neat especially since I too was a Trojan at Tara High. In return, God put on my heart to give them a copy of *Facing the Giants*. This was so all would be mutually encouraged by one another. My desire was that the coach and team could watch the movie together on the bus, so that those who knew Jesus Christ would be encouraged and that seeds might be planted into the soil of the hearts of those who may not yet know Him.

I am thankful for the blessing of the Lord Jesus Christ and for the friendship of the entire Allen family! I am also thankful for Coach Maestri and his players, for the opportunity I had to be encouraged, and then to encourage them in return.

Lesson Learned: "And let us consider how we may spur one another on toward love and good deeds, not giving up meeting together, as some are in the habit of doing, but encouraging one

183

another—and all the more as you see the Day approaching."
Hebrews 10:24-25.

But that's not the end of this story. Recently, a young friend who helps me get dressed and prepared for the day in a professional sense, asked me if I had ever seen *Facing the Giants*. I said, "Yes. In fact, I own a copy of it." So we decided to watch it together. As we did, a few things struck me that I had forgotten about.

The team and coach went through adversity. The team was losing, so doubt was creeping into the leadership ranks at the high school. The coach's car wasn't working. The family was strapped for cash. And, his wife was struggling to get pregnant in part because he was having a medical problem. But that's when he turned to the Lord Jesus in the scriptures for help. It also turned out that several others associated with the school were praying. One specific staff member, with the gift of encouragement and exhortation from the Lord, came and spoke to the coach, in essence saying this: "He has set before those He has called an Open Door that no one can shut!" See Revelation chapter 3.

(To me, this Open Door is not just about our salvation, but about the specific individual purpose that God has given to each of his anointed saints.)

The staff member went on to share a story about two farmers who were in desperate need of rain. Both farmers prayed for rain, but only one of them prepared his field to receive it. He asked the coach, "Which farmer was the best prepared? The coach replied, "The one who prepared his field." Then the staff member asked him, "Which of those two farmers are you?"

The coach, in response, began to prepare his team for victory. He had them execute a drill called the death crawl. (For those who don't know what a death crawl is, capture this in your mind's eye. Players crawl on their hands and feet, being careful not to let their knees touch the ground. They do this with a teammate on their back, lying back to back. The player who is being carried places his hands above his head and hangs on to the outside of the leader's shoulder pads until the coach says to stop.)

Lessons of Victory

After they ran through the drill, the most respected player on the team expressed doubt to his teammates and coach as to whether they could win the next Friday night's game. The coach called the player forward, as well as a teammate. But this time, the player would not only crawl with a teammate on his back, but would crawl blindfolded! The purpose of the drill was to develop the character and leadership skills of the team as a whole. The purpose of the blindfold was so the player would not predetermine with his eyes when he thought he had gone far enough, in case the coach decided to push him a little further!

In the movie, the coach got down on his knees beside his obedient crawling student and exhorted him with "Twenty more steps! You can do it!" To which the player shouted back, "It hurts! It burns!" The coach exhorted but identified with his student. "I know it hurts! I know it burns! But you can do it! Ten more steps, then five more steps. Come on! You can do it!"

The crawling player collapsed in the endzone. The coach told his player that he hadn't just crawled fifty yards, but the full length of the football field! After the player caught his breath, the coach encouraged him further: "I need you, son. This is not just about football! It's about the life ahead of you! I need you, son. Can you lead for me?" After the team leader realized his heart had just been awakened to the point of the lesson, he said yes!

This object lesson helped the team experience victory and success, even through brief moments of adversity within that success.

Lesson Learned: "Take up your cross and follow me." Mark 8:34 and Luke 9:23.

As you can see, God has caused many people, movies, stories, and events to work together for good in my life. In addition to the ones I have mentioned, I want to thank Lee Strobel, Craig Blomberg, and Josh McDowell for writing books that have influenced me greatly, such as *The Case for Christ*, *The Case for a Creator*, *The Case for Faith*, and *Evidence That Demands a Verdict*. I have listened to *The Case for Faith* seven times after initially reading it. These books

185

have inspired me to ask the Lord to lead me to those who are spiritually hungry. They have also challenged me to be content in good times and bad and to join the club, if you will, of the fellowship of Christ's sufferings.

Another important book to me is *Return of the Prodigal Son* by Henri Nouwen. Henri Nouwen went to Russia to see the Rembrandt painting called *The Prodigal Son*. He studied the way the sunlight reflected on it at different times of the day. At times, the sun highlighted the older son's anger over their father welcoming the younger son home. At other times, the sun highlighted the compassionate hands of the father as he welcomed his younger son home.

CHAPTER 38
Lessons of Salvation

Here is a poem that I wrote in 2017 as a tribute to my friend Garrett, whose father, Pat Frink, played basketball for CU. It's called "A Ship Adrift on a Dark and Stormy Sea." In the poem, the lighthouse of hope is Jesus Christ. No one can get to heaven without having a personal relationship with Jesus. He came down to earth and took the form of a baby as the Holy Spirit hovered over an imperfect woman. Through the sovereign will of God the Father, a perfect child in flesh without sin was born. Isaiah 9:6. We must receive Him as our Lord and Savior through His death and resurrection and what He accomplished on the cross. He will return again…and we will be caught up in the air to be reunited with Him. John 6:44 and John 14:6.

"A Ship Adrift on a Dark and Stormy Sea"
There is a ship adrift on a dark and stormy sea. But there is a lighthouse of hope calling all ships to come in! One ship could be you and another could be me.

There was a man born in the town of Bethlehem which means "house of bread."
He declared: "I am the bread of life, whoever comes to me will never go hungry"… John 6:35
Do you know him?
He has spiritual food that can satisfy your soul.

There is a ship adrift on a dark and stormy sea. But there is a lighthouse of hope calling all ships to come in! One ship could be you and another could be me.

Your mind could be tangled in a lie from what the world wants its residents to believe.
Are you haunted by worry but thirsty and wanting to be free?
You could be ensnared by your anger or the wounds of your past.
Maybe you feel hopeless and when you look down you see that you are going nowhere because you just discovered that what you built your house upon is really sinking sand.

187

There is a ship adrift on a dark and stormy sea. But there is a lighthouse of hope calling all ships to come in! One ship could be you and another could be me.

There is a man known as a lighthouse calling to lead you out of the darkness who says, "Whoever follows me will never walk in darkness but will have the light of life." John 8:12.
Do you know him?
Are you hungry?
Are you thirsty?
Are you looking for security?
Are you looking for a home?

There is a ship adrift on a dark and stormy sea. But there is a lighthouse of hope calling all ships to come in! One ship could be you and another could be me.

Now there was a man named Jesus who came to the town of Sychar in Samaria and sat down by Jacob's Well to rest.
(And the disciples were not with him because they went into town to buy food.)
When a Samaritan woman came to the well to draw water this man named Jesus asked, "Will you give me a drink?"

What you may not know now about this story is that this simple question could be a problem.
This simple question could raise a stink!
And leave a clog in the Jew and Samaritan relational kitchen sink!
(Because Jews do not associate with Samaritans! It was considered a shameful thing to do.)

So she replied to Jesus with surprise in her voice.
"But you are a Jew! And I am a Samaritan woman!
How can I give you a drink?"

Jesus answered her, "If you knew the gift of GOD.
If you knew who was sitting on this historic and ancient sod.
You would have asked him, and he would have given you living water."

188

"Sir," she said, with zest and energy building in her voice!
"But you have nothing to draw with and this well is deep.
Where can you get this living water?"
Are you greater than our father Jacob who gave us this well?"

Jesus answered her, "Everyone who drinks this water will be thirsty again.
But whoever drinks the water I give them will never be thirsty again."
Yes, "whoever drinks the water I give them, it will become in them a spring welling up to eternal life."

Again she replied with excitement, but this time a sense of awe colored her words.
"Sir! Give me this living water so that I will not get thirsty and have to keep coming to this well to draw water!"

There is a ship adrift on a dark and stormy sea. But there is a lighthouse of hope calling all ships to come in. One ship could be you and another could be me.

So Jesus asker her, "Go call your husband and come back."
"I have no husband," she replied.

Jesus said to her, "You are right when you say you have no husband. The fact is you have had five husbands and the man you are now with is not your husband. What you have said is quite true."

Still with astonishment in her voice, the woman said, "I can see that you are a prophet.
Our ancestors worshipped on this mountain but you Jews claim that the place where we must worship is Jerusalem."

"Woman," Jesus replied, "Believe me! A time is coming when you will neither worship God on this mountain or in Jerusalem.
You Samaritans worship what you do not know. We worship what we do know because salvation is from the Jews.
Yet a time is coming and has now come when the true worshippers will worship the father in the spirit and in truth for they are the

kind of worshippers the father seeks.
God is spirit and his worshippers must worship him in spirit and
truth. "

Then with still greater focus she replied, "I know that the Messiah
(called Christ) is coming and when he comes he will tell us
everything."

Then Jesus declared as the disciples were coming back.
"I, the one speaking to you, am he!"

Then leaving her water jar as though she were no longer interested
in earthly water,
she went back into town saying:
"Come see a man who told me everything I ever did!"

And then, as if to offer an invitation she exclaimed, "Could this be
the messiah?"

So they came out of the town and made their way toward him.
(From John 4:1-30).

There is a ship adrift on a dark and stormy sea. But there is a
lighthouse of hope calling all ships to come in! Are you hungry?
Are you thirsty? Come! Bring it all to him and leave it there.

Because...
One ship could be you and another could be me.
One ship could be you and another could be me.
One ship could be you and another could be me.

I often listen to David Jeremiah's teachings on the radio. I remember
one in particular about David's anointing as king. David made a lot
of mistakes and there were heavy prices to pay, but God never gave
up on him. He was a leader and so am I.

In 2017, as I was getting ready for a friend's funeral, I was listening
to David Jeremiah talk about the difference between physical hunger
and spiritual hunger. He was going through a series on the Beatitudes
in the Book of Matthew. He began describing how when someone is
physically hungry, they eat until they are full. However, when

someone is dry and unmotivated to spend time with God, the key is to force-feed yourself, or press in to God, as Andy frequently says.

The term "force-feed" helped me figure out what Andy means. It looks like this: Keep praying and ask God to speak to you. Ask God for help to overcome dry times. At some point, when we keep knocking at the door, so to speak (Rev. 3:20), God reveals some portion of scripture.

When you are a Christian, this happens through the Holy Spirit. The Spirit illumines a word, verse, or passage with the deeper meaning He wants you to grasp. When this takes place, you have a sense of hunger, yet instead of being made full, as is the case after you eat physical food, the spiritual food of God's insight is highlighted in your soul and you become MORE hungry!

The pastor at the funeral, David Kummer, referenced two things that the Holy Spirit illuminated for me. The first was from Proverbs 3:5-6. The passage exhorts us to trust the Lord with our whole heart, then acknowledge Him in all our ways, and He will make our paths straight. I memorized this verse years ago with Jeff and Pam Giles. To me, back then, the word "acknowledge" meant to say hello to someone who was being kind, to smile back at someone who was taking the time to smile at you, or to wave at someone who was waving at you.

But the pastor said the Hebrew translation of the word "acknowledge" used here means to know God intimately! This is done with the Spirit's help. It is not enough just to know about Him. This was a profound insight to me. The Holy Spirit illumined this word and this moment as an invitation to go deeper with Him!

Two days later, with all of this still on my mind, I prayed through Isaiah chapter 55 twice very slowly. I tried to read the chapter as if God were speaking directly to me, since God was trying to speak directly to His people through the prophet Isaiah even before it was recorded in the scriptures. Again, the Holy Spirit was active in the process of my reading and prayer.

In Isaiah 55, He invited all who are thirsty to come buy wine and milk at no cost. He also said, "Why spend money on what does not satisfy?" I'm learning how to be content while attempting to obey Him in word, deed, and prayer.

What God communicated to me was this idea: Lift up your heart to me! No matter how many times you have to do it, lift up your heart. Lift up the pain and surrender! What is your heart longing for?

I could sense that God was asking me to be totally honest. I had been hurting since the divorce of my parents. I had memories of the pain between them. I wanted to fix it. (I mean nothing personal towards my step-parents. I am grateful, looking back on all they did for me. But I wanted to fix what I did not have the power to fix. I am still slowly grasping this.)

Near the end of Isaiah 55, God talked about the myrtle tree. The myrtle tree grows in Israel, California, and Oregon. It starts out as a bush but grows strong, sturdy, and tall. Myrtle trees grow close together with other myrtle trees. Weather, wind, and hard experiences, as well as good times, affect the color of the wood, which you can see when the wood is cut to make furniture. The myrtle tree is a description of the church body working together as one unit to help each other through the unique gifts and differences of each member.

Another concept in Isaiah 55 is that because we belong to God, we can call out to those we do not know. People we don't know will come running to us because they see something in us they desire. They will do this because we are the Lord's renowned.

As you read this, I can use your prayers that I will remain thirsty to seek the Lord.

Lesson Learned: As the Lord says in Isaiah 55, His ways are not my ways. As high as the heavens are above me, so are His ways far above mine.

Some scripture verses that are important to me are 1st John 1:9, Proverbs 3:5-6, and Philippians 4:6-7. The first verse I memorized was Psalm 51:17, written by King David who struggled with his thought life and with moral purity, just like me. "God is delighted in a broken spirit and a broken and contrite heart." In other words, God thinks highly of humble ways and humble tears!

Here is a poem I wrote about this very thing, based on Psalm 51:17.

"Make Us Holy in our Tears"
Lord, when the world in its foolishness shouts,
"Big Boys Don't Cry! Big Boys Don't Cry!"
Cause us to lift up our hands in Praise!

As you show us a different purpose or paint for us a portrait
Of the HOLY reasons, how and why.
May a Hallelujah Chorus be heard
From the valleys to the mountain tops!
How great thou Lord is your love!
How great oh Lord is your name!

In heartbreak, contrition, or victory Lord!
For your glory Lord,
Receive our tears.

For you have given us your righteousness Lord,
When you exchanged your life
For ours;

Oh Lord, you have saved us for your namesake!
You have saved us by your Covenant!
You have saved us because you delight in US!

You have rewarded us according to your vast unfailing love!
This is a precious gift you have given to us and that you have imparted to us!
You delight in a broken spirit and in a broken and contrite heart.

So, when the salt of our tears touches our lips,
May the praise that comes from the humble act of them taste sweet to you oh Lord!

Make us humble,
Make us pure,
Make us HOLY
In your sight oh Lord!

When we stumble,
When we sin,
Bring forth a willing heart
That searches and probes,
From a sincere confession,
From deep within!

Bring forth praise from our mouths,
And a new song from our lips!
Create in us a clean heart O Lord!

Jesus, you alone are worthy!
You alone deserve the praise!
When Life deals a blow and we are on our knees in tears and
cannot stand!
Let us be willing to be willing to give it to you!
Let us consider it pure joy when we go through trials of many
kinds! James 1:3-5.

Give us humble words to pray when our longings are not met!
And in those times when we vent our anger to you. Bring us back!
Bring us back! To a place where we can clean up the mess and be
restored! I love you Lord!

I love you Lord!

When we are willing to be willing, empower us to pray for your
will, and not ours to be done! Cause us to praise you and lift up
humble hands!

Let the greatness of your name be known throughout the Earth;
From the Valleys to the mountain tops Jesus!

For you are our salvation!
You are our reward!
Let us sing, in season, songs of gladness and of overwhelming Joy!

For you allow the weak things in the world to shame the strong and you bring the foolish things of the world to shame the wise. 1 Corinthians 1:25-31

Sanctify us all! Lord Jesus, sanctify us all!
In Victory or Brokenness,
Let our humble tears forever Proclaim the greatness of your name!
Let our humble tears forever Proclaim your amazing and steadfast love!

By the power of your Victory on the cross oh Lord,
Our defeats have been redeemed and our victories have been Won!

Sanctify us all! Lord Jesus, sanctify us all!
Purify us with Holy Fire oh Lord!

Let praise and glory be given to your holy name forever oh Lord!
For it is you and you alone!
Who sits on the throne,
Amen! And amen!

Create in us a clean heart,
And you delight in a broken spirit and a broken and contrite heart.

CHAPTER 39
Lessons of Singleness

Very recently, in July of 2018, God brought me to terms with my singleness. Maybe I didn't see the truth before because I didn't want to. Or maybe I just wasn't ready to. I think the answer lies somewhere in the middle.

God is the author of marriage. Even then, sometimes a marriage doesn't work for reasons only God and the two involved persons know, but a tearing of what God has woven together takes place, which creates pain, just like death creates pain. Something that God put together is dying or has died. Only God can work with us through the options to heal.

Being single is a gift! Being married is a gift! If He wants us to be married the choice is His! If He wants us to be single the choice is His! He is the Lord. He is my Lord. He doesn't love me any more or any less than He did when he created me!

For the longest time, I was putting the sign "marriage" across the chest of every able-bodied girl I met. I was putting my desire to belong into the vacuum where only God rightfully belongs. In doing this, I was in denial about my disability. I had a deep wound because of loneliness and the festering that began when I heard my parents arguing. I was unable to affect the choices they were making. I tried to fill the void by self-medicating. I just wanted the ache to go away.

I spent many years doing the very thing that scripture tells us not to do. If you are not married, do not look for a wife. 1 Corinthians 7:27. Give that responsibility to the Lord. Let Him fulfill His purpose for you. In contrast, Proverbs 18:22 says that if a man finds a wife, he finds a good thing and receives honor and blessing from the Lord!

Let me put these two verses side by side. If I express my desire to have a wife and it is part of God's ultimate plan for my life, it will happen and I don't need to think about it any further. If it is God's will, it is as good as done! However, if it is not His will for me, no matter how hard I try, rest assured I will be frustrated in the attempt! This is where the lordship of Jesus Christ and the sovereignty of God join together as separate persons in the godhead yet as one God, so to speak.

For years I was hurting myself mentally and psychologically because I was trying to take matters into my own hands. Tim Keller, in the book he wrote with his wife called *The Meaning of Marriage*, referred to being overly-focused on, overvaluing, or undervaluing marriage rather than trusting God's ultimate answer: yes, no, or wait. It is a pathology to not view singleness and marriage as equally valuable.

God has taught me that what a man fails to learn, he is destined to repeat. When I would view myself as less than the way God views me, I was playing God. My attitude was in effect saying that my standards were higher than God's. I am not perfect, but Christ is perfect, and I will be judged righteous by God through the blood that Jesus shed on the cross.

He desires to effect change in us through the power of His Holy Spirit. The following verses are examples of what God has been trying to get across to me since the age of 30. First, the story of Abraham and Isaac in Genesis 22:1-18. Then Hebrews 6:13-19. And finally, Joshua 4:1-18.

Jesus Christ is a longsuffering, loving, and patient God. His heart is deep with compassion. He does not desire for us to suffer (without Him), but rather, to have eternal life! 2 Peter 3:9

Lesson Learned: For me, trusting God concerning the gift of singleness has been easier said than done, but hearing Chuck Swindoll's series, *Hope for Those Who Doubt*, was a gift from the Lord in this regard. God sends us what we need.

The following poem was inspired by the music of Bryan Duncan and some of my own poetry. I wrote it in 2017.

"I Love You, Jesus"
"I love you Jesus. I can't wait for the day when I can love you perfectly! When my sin nature is out of the way and gone! All I can

do for now is rejoice that I am standing in your grace, even as I sit here in my wheelchair!

I love you Lord Jesus. You bring new friends into my life like flowers that spring from the ground to greet the sunlight and the spring rain.

You teach me how to love you with my life. Jesus, you pick me up when I fall short. I feel so lonely sometimes. I turn to my own devices. I try to fix things with my own tools. But then I realize, not long after that, it just isn't going to work. All I have to do is turn and face you! All I have to do is acknowledge that I have made a mess and only you can redeem what has been done and make it right.

I love you Jesus, I love you! You are the only love that truly understands me! It should be obvious to me since you created me. But when I forget, all I have to do is turn to you and love you with honesty and love you with my life!

You love me in my laughter.
You love me in my confusion.
You love me in the tears that fall!

You alone are my Lord and Savior.
You alone comfort me in my loneliness! When I receive the comfort of a friend, it is you that brought her. It is you that brought him! And it is you that is there in the middle of the two of them!

You brought me to a place of loneliness so that I might discover you in a deeper way, when I try to find my identity in something other than you, forgetting all the while that you are The Giver of all good gifts and that I push you or crowd you out in my confusion or my anger.

It is you who forgives my pride! It is you who hears my humble confession and cry.
It is you who washes my eyes with my own tears!
You make my eyes, the window to my soul, clear again."

CHAPTER 40
Lessons of Gratitude

Today, in 2018, I want to bring you up to date. I am still the director at Cornerstone Home. I served on the Patient Advocacy Board at the Inner City Health Center for six years and became a member of the ICHC Board of Directors in late 2017 by the grace of God. Over the years, I've been able to raise funds for projects important to me, such as TRYAD events like the Thank Christ Dinner (to celebrate Thanksgiving and Christmas at the same time), our Easter Fellowship, and our annual summer retreat in the mountains through a fundraiser called Stroll & Roll. I have assisted with Run for the Door, one of the four major fundraisers benefitting Open Door Ministries. I've filled communion cups for Chris Hooper. I've helped make CDs of Andy's sermons. I put a team together to help victims of Hurricane Katrina.

As I write this, I have just been given the opportunity to become the Chairman of the Elders at Open Door. I want to be a better listener. I don't feel qualified, but God qualifies the called. I want to encourage my brothers within the framework of the gifts they possess. I want to listen well, to point out their strengths and the assets of their viewpoints, so they can knit those together. I want to be sensitive to timetables and deadlines. In this way I will do my job well.

I once told my sister, Lana, that I wished I had a Master's degree like she has. She said, "Randy, who is it that is always encouraging us to set our sights on Jesus Christ and the cross? It's you! You have a Master's degree in LIFE!" When I first joined the ICHC Patient Advocacy Board, I called her and told her I had gotten my Master's in Life. Later, I asked her, "When are you going to get your PhD?" She said, "Randy, give me a break! I need some rest. I just got a Master's degree and now you want to know if I'm getting a PhD!" But it didn't take her long. She started pursuing and soon got a PhD. After I became an elder at our church, I called her and told I got my PhD in Life!

Lesson Learned: I'm so thankful for my family and friends. I'm learning that I am loved deeply, not only by them, but by the Lord, more deeply than I know. I am not defined by what I do or fail to do. And I am not defined by who I know or by what I possess. I am defined by who I am in the eyes of God. God gives us the qualifications we need as we go along through the Holy Spirit. Romans 8:28. He redeems our weaknesses, cashing them in, in a sense, to make our weaknesses His strength.

One of the most meaningful metaphors of my life is the song "Climb Every Mountain" from *The Sound of Music*. I recently learned that my friend Lyn was taking a family trip to Europe, including Austria. I asked if she would be willing to look for a souvenir in Austria related to the Von Trapp family for me.

I remember watching *The Sound of Music* on television with both sets of parents over the years. As a child, I sang "Climb Every Mountain" as a solo. In the beginning, the song was just a song and the story was just a story. But the more I watched the movie, the song and story started resonating in my soul. The movie was a portrait of freedom from the adversity so many people faced during World War II. My grandparents persevered through the war before any of my parents, biological or otherwise, were born. The song, written by Oscar Hammerstein II, was a metaphor, a challenge, and an exhortation to look deeper into the beauty of the story. It can be sung as a prayer in the strength of Christ Jesus.

 "Climb every mountain,
Search high and low,
Follow every byway,
Every path you know.
Climb every mountain,
Ford every stream,
Follow every rainbow,
'Til you find your dream."

Lyn indeed sent me the souvenir book and I was so touched to receive it. Then I was even more moved by the story of the real life Von Trapp family. The woman named Maria searched to find and embrace her true calling in life. She then overcame the adversity she faced with her husband and young children from her husband's previous marriage to escape Hitler's occupation of Austria. After hearing my caregiver read this book to me, I had a newfound appreciation for my dad and stepmom as well as my mom and stepfather, for their quest to love my sisters and me, put food on the table, and live a life of love.

As the movie concluded, I heard the lyrics of "Climb Every Mountain." They pierced my heart and I was moved to tears with profound gratitude as I reflected on all the obstacles in my life, including the recent surrender of my desire to be married and to define life as a success by insisting that my longing to be married be met.

Lesson Learned: Climbing every mountain, for me, is not about trying harder. It is about surrender on an even deeper level to my Lord and Savior Jesus Christ. It is not about what the Lord wants me to prove to Him. Instead it is about what He wants to reveal to me. He will be faithful to me not because I have done anything special, but because of His loving covenant all the way through from the old to the new. He will provide, He alone, for His own name's sake!

My 60th birthday, February 28, 2018, was a big landmark. I have experienced deep pain and deep joy over the past sixty years. I have learned much. I have given my life to my Savior and Lord, Jesus Christ, so my eternity is secure! But for the rest of my life, whether that be days or decades, I have dreams! One dream has been fulfilled, and that is the writing of this autobiography. Another is yet to be fulfilled, and that is my dream to build a home for disabled women, similar to Cornerstone, or for a home for disabled men and women to live together in community.

I think there are yet more lessons to be written from the bottom of the stairs before I see the Lord face to face with a new body and eternity with Him! So until then, "I do not consider myself yet to have taken hold of it. But one thing I do: Forgetting what is behind and straining toward what is ahead, I press on toward the goal to win the prize for which God has called me heavenward in Christ Jesus." Philippians 3:13-14

Thank you, Lord, for the gifts you have given me. Please grant me your favor to continue to do more of the same, if it is your will. Please multiply the strength and courage of my brothers and sisters in the tasks you have given us all. For your glory and honor alone. Amen.

Thank you for taking the time to read this book I hope it was a blessing to you and that it will continue to be a blessing as you think about it! May the peace of Jesus Christ bless you with the richness of His love and compassion. 2 Corinthians 1:3-11.

Sincerely,

Your Brother in Christ, Randy Milliken

POSTSCRIPT

From Randy: I started thinking about writing this book in the fall of 2016. I thought about taking a class in Computer Voice Activation Technology a second time, since it had been more than twenty years since I had last tried to use this technology and I had forgotten how it worked. But after thinking about this, I realized I had another problem to solve. How was I going to take classes to learn about the software if I had to change clothes three times a day due to incontinence issues?

Well, last summer I had lunch with Debbie Johnson. She brought me a copy of her book, *A Pocketful of Seeds*, so I asked her if she would help me with a book I wanted to write! She said yes…encouraging me to send her my story by smart phone voice-activated email.

Approximately one year later, in August of 2018, after many hours of recording my stories and Debbie's editing, we're finished! I actually wrote this book using my Galaxy S7 Android smartphone. Technology has come a long way between my birth in 1958 and today (2018)!

To support the future home for disabled people in Denver, Colorado, contact Open Door Ministries, www.odmdenver.org and inquire about the dream projects I have described in this book. 303-830-2201.

From Debbie: From time to time since the 90's, Randy and I have gotten together to catch up on life. I'm always inspired by his faith and overcoming spirit. At that lunch last summer, he started telling me some stories I had never heard before. I said, "Dude, you need to write a book!" And as Randy said, the rest is history.

The hardest part has been figuring out where to end it. He's only 60. There will be many more stories for him to experience and lessons to learn. Actually, an eternity's worth. If he doesn't end up writing a sequel, I suppose we'll just meet up in heaven from time to time and catch up.

He owes me a foot race anyway.

Made in the USA
San Bernardino, CA
13 December 2018